Le Charcutier ANGLAIS

MARC FREDERIC

At the start of writing this book I thought I might fall at the first hurdle given my fear of working with the written word. Not only did I pass the first hurdle without incident, I managed to complete the book. However, I can say this was only possible due to the help, support and patience that had been shown to me from my family and close friends.

Then came the professional help from the team at Pentacor book design, two of whom happen to be vegetarians (what barriers they must have faced in compiling this meat book), who made the book what it is today. Without them and their tenacity, patience and resilience the book would not be what it is, and that is a record of small chapters in my life with real time recipes for future foodies, cooks and charcutiers to use.

The book I hope offers a base line for newcomers to use without experiencing any failure. My ultimate aim in writing this book is to make you smile, whether that is through my true stories or through the recipes you may try.

If you're smiling, then the food will take care of itself!

Marc-Frederic

CONTENTS

FOREWORD

Marc-Frederic is by far the most knowledgeable and experienced Englishman I know when it comes to *charcuterie* and his experience with game is just outstanding. It is a breath of fresh air to read a cookbook written straight from the heart, the honesty and the humour of the man is found throughout his book. *Le Charcutier Anglais* is indeed a rare insight into the world of *charcuterie* not only does it offer you the "feel good factor" his book will both amuse and educate you at the same time.

Franck Pontais
Author, *Terrines and Verrines*

INTRODUCTION

Ah! The book, the book, the book – will I ever write a book? I don't think so, but I will give it a good go, if only to stop those who badger me to do so sounding like a stuck record. After writing the first couple of lines the thought of a whole book is already shaking me to the core, because I am fearful of even the simple task of filling in forms (they make me turn all phobic and blotchy as if suffering from an allergy). Even though I am an excellent speller I am unable to decipher my own joined-up writing, so I gave up as a teenager and now just print if I am forced to write anything. My signature is not legible either – it looks as if I am trying to hide or disguise who I am. There! I have already divulged a personal weakness that will surprise those who know me, given my outward confidence.

The idea of leaving my children a legacy or an insight to part of my life is appealing, but writing a biography for others to read certainly is not. I'm far too private a person, and besides, my children do not need to know many of the things that have happened in my life. Not that there is anything sinister in my closet, I would just prefer them to remember the happy times we have all shared, and to use some of those times to help them in their own lives. They have really made my life a happy one – thanks kids!

Allowing others to access some of my *charcuterie* recipes is one way to approach this book. You see, I have never been shy about sharing recipes or techniques, much to the disgust of some in the trade. Those who do show their disgust are not on my Christmas card list nor in my circle of friends, so I have nothing to lose there! For far too many years recipes have been jealously guarded by some as if they were magicians within the Magic Circle, but eventually even our own Government release secrets; it may take them 40 years, but they do share them in the end.

Probably due to my fear of the written word I have read very few books in my lifetime, my first was *The Belstone Fox* and thereafter my reading has been solely restricted to cook books or maybe the odd instruction pamphlet on how to use a certain piece of equipment safely. Throughout my childhood I was given books for Christmas by a favourite aunt, and to this day I have not even opened the front cover of any of them, except to read her sentiments. I could never bring myself to tell her about my fear thinking that I might sound silly. Yet I now possess a good collection of cookery books to which I refer frequently and with ease, in particular to those with great illustrations.

So, "How on earth did you ever get through school?" you ask. Well it was difficult at times, but volunteering to do the teacher's errands was one way of avoiding English lessons. Lessons other than English were OK particularly such practical ones as Metalwork and Woodwork, and when Domestic Science came along I was in my element learning how to make Banana Bread. Oh! The joy of being clever enough to mix all these wonderful yet simple ingredients together, placing the loaf in an oven to bake for a while, and then waiting for it to cool before rushing home at the end of the day with what seemed like the FA Cup in my hands! Mum, Dad and my two sisters praised my culinary efforts, but it was the joy of seeing my family gorging themselves that made the biggest impression on me. The noise they all made whilst enjoying each and every morsel of that first loaf has stayed with me to this very day. Their mouths were slowly twisting and turning looking like a mix of Wallace and Gromit characters and choristers with O-shaped mouths singing; "Hmmmmmmm… Oh yes, Oh yes, yes, Yes, YES … Did you really make this?" They sounded more like a Meg Ryan moment (*When Harry met Sally*) than the verse of a song, but it became the reaction I have achieved many thousand times since and one for which I still strive today. Of course Wallace and Gromit weren't around then, but all the

same that is the picture I have in my mind when I think back to those early days. I grew up in the era of Graham Kerr the 'Galloping Gourmet'. Do you remember him savouring those tasting moments when he sat down with a guest from the audience after conjuring up food you thought was only for kings and queens?

When we were due to leave school my classmates and I had to visit an Employment Officer at the Labour Exchange, as the Job Centre is now known, to discuss our futures. I had to tell this stranger what my strengths and weaknesses were so he could decide what type of employment I should seek. I recall telling him how much I enjoyed cooking at school; how it was the only subject that stopped me from playing truant, and the only topic that made me punctual and attentive in class without disrupting the teacher. This Employment Officer having heard my interest in food concluded his findings by refusing to enrol me in the local Catering College! I was devastated by this news and he then added insult to injury by saying I was not bright enough to attend the college and ought to pursue a career as a painter and decorator (for which he had several apprentice positions available!). I ignored his advice and never visited him again as I knew by then that I would have to make my own way in life.

I did visit the Catering College though; I took a bus ride and reached the college in time to watch all the newcomers take their places inside the building whilst I walked around the grounds torturing myself with thoughts of what it would be like in there learning that wonderful craft. I cried with the pain of being excluded from this facility and every day for a week I took the same bus ride as those lucky students, as if I were one of them. I even found myself bellowing at one student for being late for class as I took my place outside in the grounds. Eventually a good downpour of rain stopped me standing outside the college and I woke up to the fact I was never going to get inside as a student. So, for the very last time, I walked around the building and peered through each window before turning my back and setting off in search of my future.

The recipes I have chosen to include in this book are the ones that have brought my family and me the most fun, and are recipes I feel are important to both the budding *charcutier* and the family man. Last but not least, I hope these recipes are ones that will inspire you to be both creative and judgemental, for then I will know that writing the book has been worthwhile. Treat this book as a quick guide to *charcuterie*, one without complexities; one that will make you laugh; one that will make you feel "I can do that" and one that will set you well on the road to discovery.

Whilst I have your attention I need to clarify who I really am; you see my real name is Mark Frederick Berry. Amongst my friends I have always been known as Big Mark, as there were two Marks in our group of friends and, yes, I am the taller and heavier of the two (Little Mark by the way is now approximately 18stone, 6ft tall and a gamekeeper in Yorkshire!). Whilst living in France, it soon became apparent that the French were unable to pronounce the name 'Mark' without it sounding like 'Mac'. However, they could pronounce doubled-barrelled names much more easily and, having heard that my British friends refer to me as Big Mark, they started to call me Big Mac. This made me feel like a double beef burger with sour gherkins and relish and the name often caused much laughter and ridicule – given that I am an artisan in the meat trade! I then discovered that the French found it easier to add my middle name, Frederick, to Mark thus creating Marc-Frederic. This combination soon caught on amongst my French friends and very quickly I became known as Marc-Frederic, *Le Charcutier Anglais* and the rest is history as they say.

Well, that's enough introduction, I hope you are tempted enough to turn a few more pages on which you will find not just recipes but also flashbacks to some of my experiences. And where I can, I will use real-time humour to giddy you along because humour is the most important ingredient I use and one that is stocked in plenty in my larder!

Marc-Frederic
Dawlish, Devon, England
January 2011

UTENSILS

It seems daft writing about utensils (or implements as some prefer to call them), or at least it did until I thought about it, because if you are going to follow a recipe that, for example, tells you to use a wooden spoon to stir a mixture, do you go rushing out to buy one like those smitten by 'Delia Mania' (or 'Martha Mania' if you are reading this book in the USA)? Or, worse still, avoid cooking the recipe because you don't have one. Of course you don't, you use your common sense and adapt; I would even use the poker from the hearth if I had to. (*Thinking about it, where is that poker? Oh yes, I left it in the plastic bucket with my homemade mead, did I say* **"plastic bucket?"** *Oh S**T!*)

And besides, if you only intend to attempt a recipe once, then ignore the 'helpful tips' and just get on with it – your results will be the same. Your arm may ache afterwards if your recipe required a lot of stirring and you might wish you had bought that state-of-the-art blender, but – eh! You are here to enjoy the proceeds and you will!

Right! Let's get into the process of *charcuterie*. What do we need? We need to think about the butchery process first and that requires the following tools that will make butchering simpler:

- MEAT SAW
- BONING KNIFE
- STEEL
- STEAK KNIFE
- STANLEY™ KNIFE

I always try to find easier ways to do things without compromising quality, but those of you who are already skilled in butchery know that a boning knife alone could do all the work. I would rather use carbon steel knives than stainless steel ones, but nowadays they are hard to find.

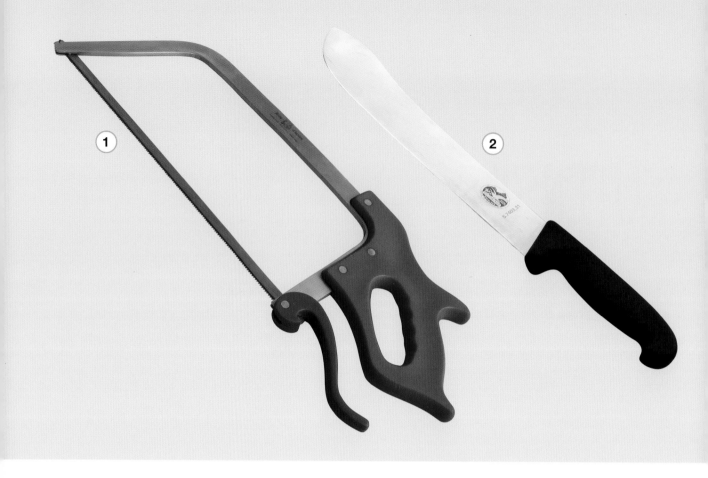

MEAT SAW ① Currently I use a King Charles™ saw with an 18-inch blade but a 20+-inch blade would be preferable, since getting through the larger breeds of pig that are normally used for *charcuterie* is difficult with a shorter blade. Remember though, when changing or replacing a blade, e.g. after washing it, that the teeth of the blade face forwards.

STEAK KNIFE ② I use a Swiss-made Victorinox™ with a 12-inch blade. The German company, F Dick™ also make good knives.

BONING KNIFE ③ I use a French one, and I would like to emphasise the need to ensure you get a flexible knife that is stamped 'flexi' on the blade. This will help you when 'boning out' and be ideal for getting in and around all those tight spaces associated with cartilage and small-boned areas.

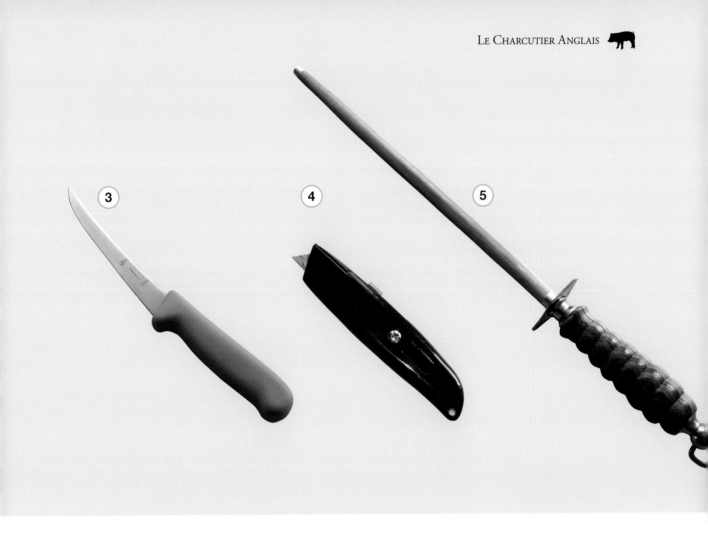

STANLEY™ KNIFE ④ No, we are not about to digress and start some DIY or lay a piece of carpet, but I do think this is a useful knife to have around because you can set the depth of its blade, thus enabling you to achieve perfect scoring on your pork. Set the blade against the depth of fat and remember to score over the edges of your rind. If you are tying up a roasting joint the butchers' string will hold the meat together better if it can follow the narrow cuts you have made whilst scoring the skin. (Invest in coloured string and your handiwork will look even better!) Special scoring knives are available with four or more fixed interchangeable blades, but I have never felt the need to buy or use one of them.

STEEL ⑤ Last but not least is a humble tool that should never be overlooked or under-estimated. The steel is the 'heel' of butchery and is essential for keeping a fine edge on your knives. I cannot emphasise enough how often you must use your steel.

> **Remember this!**
> It is a blunt knife that will cut you before a sharp knife will.
>
> Just to make sure you heard me, I am going to repeat that statement…
> **REMEMBER THIS!**
> **It is a blunt knife that will cut you before a sharp knife will.**

13

I know you heard me that time, so let's carry on. The way to use a steel is to take it by the handle and hold it vertically (as if taking hold of a porcelain draught beer pump handle in the bar of your local pub), then apply a little pressure so the 'nose' of the steel is embedded into your cutting table or butchers block, now place your knife flat against the steel and tilt it at a 30° angle. (If, like me, you don't understand angles, hold your steel with the handle facing 12 o'clock and tilt the back of your knife between 1 and 2 o'clock.) Draw your knife down one side of the steel and again down the other side, covering the full length of your blade. Do this several times and your knife will keep its edge well. Do not forget to repeat this process time after time after time. (I wasn't referring to last orders in the pub; we're off that subject now!) I must say at this point you will know when you are proficient at sharpening knives when the sound of sharpening blades is like an Edward Scissorhands topiary class.

top to bottom: A *hachoir*, pie moulds and a grinder attached to my Kitchen-Aid™.

Other tools and equipment that are needed, or at least useful for *charcuterie* include:

HACHOIR A double curved blade with a wooden handle is what you see today, this tool with it's rocking motion can chop meats down to a fine mince. In years past *hachoirs* were so large that, like see-saws, they were operated by two people.

SCALES It is better to have metric scales today as most recipes are in metric, or have been converted from imperial measurements.

PIE MOULDS Large and small round moulds for pork pies, oblong veal and ham moulds for making Gala and Ascot pies, and a large round cake tin, the type with the quick release sides (known in America as a 'spring-form pan') to use when making the French *Pâté de Paque* (Easter Pie).

GRINDER Anything from the clamp-on and hand-operated Porkett™ mincer to a household electric blender with mincer attachments will make your life easier. The more *charcuterie* you intend to practise the better the mincer you will want to have, and one with sausage-making funnels is a real bonus. Of course, a professional grinder would be the

All cut up

When I was a child we were a very poor family as I recall and although we had very few possessions, we did have a well used steel in our home kitchen. From time-to-time Dad would conjure up an animal carcass, which would be delivered mysteriously covered in muslin to us during the dark hours and hung up outside in our back yard. These were special times full of excitement and as I was the only lad in the family I would be allowed to help in the butchering of whatever animal was revealed from beneath the woven 'shroud'.

I was given the task of sharpening the knives, for this was 'man's work' my dad would say. I felt 10ft tall, but I did not use the steel – because this was a special job, Dad would say I should use the front doorstep. Yes, you heard right, because 'up North' in Lancashire doorsteps were made from stone with bevelled edges ideal for knife sharpening. A clean-scrubbed, freshly chalked doorstep was a sure sign that inside that house lived a house-proud woman who kept everything spick and span. I remember the Rag and Bone men who frequented our back streets with their horses and carts bellowing at you to "Bring out your old rags", in exchange for lumps of grey chalk. These 'rewards' enabled you to whiten the edge of your doorstep after its weekly mopping. A job my sisters would do for pocket money after knocking on doors to ask those who did not have the time or the inclination to do their own even if they could: "Do your step missis? Only a threppny bit!"

Dad was a very shrewd man, he knew that sending me out to the front doorstep to sharpen those knives would prompt our very nosey neighbours to ask (read in a Lancashire accent here) "What yer doing lad?" I would respond, lightning quick and with great pride, "I've got t'sharpen knives, 'cos I'm helping Dad cut up pig".

Mrs Howard the fat lady from next door would be the first to ask me. She was always sitting on her doorstep watching the world pass by dressed in her floral pinny. This would be rolled up – displaying her inner thighs full of cellulite (corned beef legs) and her big bloomers. Often she would be sucking on a piece of jellied cowheel, for she had no teeth, and only wore her dentures if she ever left the house or had visitors (she looked liked Les Dawson in drag). The sucking noises she made whilst devouring her gelatinous feast were one thing, but the movement of her face as she made her way round the knuckle joint was a sight not easily forgotten – French kissing at it's very best is how I'd describe it! (Even though still a juvenile I knew that when the time came to practise my kissing technique it would not be with a jellied cow heel or on a fat neighbour with no teeth!). After asking me what I was doing she'd shout in her best vernacular to her youngest daughter "Suuuuusan, Susan bring me teeth I'm off over road t'see Mrs Riley". And in due course all the women in the street would turn up at our house with their willow baskets, only to leave some moments later with fresh pork wrapped in used newspaper and saying; "We'll settle up with you on Friday then George." – Friday being payday for the workers in those days. Payday also meant that all the blokes would be in the pub and Dad knew this, so whilst we as a family were enjoying our share of the pork, Dad would be contentedly collecting his debts in the pub. Bloody clever my Dad! (He died of cirrhosis of the liver when he was 59 and far too young to have left us. I could jokingly say here; "That was a lot of butchered pigs Dad!" And if he were looking down, I know that he would be laughing with me – you see, that is something else I have to thank him for, my sense of humour.)

left to right: A sausage filler attachment on my Kitchen-Aid™ and a wok, showing how the rack of lamb fits to the curved sides.

best sort; one that is at least 750 watt or more is ideal for the small-scale user. (I have to tell you quickly here, if you promise not to copy! I was once at home using my Kitchen-Aid™ and grinder attachment to mince some pork when I overloaded it and burned the clutch out. Eager to finish what I was doing, I found a G-clamp to secure my electric drill to my work surface and I ran my Kitchen- Aid™ grinder from my drill to mince the remaining pork.)

SAUSAGE FILLER This could simply be a plastic funnel or spout that fits onto your electric mincer attachment. For the more serious *charcutier* an 8ltr vertical or horizontal filler with a hand-crank mechanism or even a large, electrically powered hydraulic filler system is suitable. I prefer using a horizontal filler, one that I can operate almost as quickly as a hydraulic system. My horizontal sausage filler accompanies me on all my travels, even when I go on holiday, much to my family's annoyance!

TERRINES Various shapes and sizes.

VERRINES Glassware of various sorts.

FRYING PAN A heavy-duty, cast-iron skillet is the type I most prefer.

CHOPPING BOARDS Wooden ones are still my personal choice, made from beech if possible for ease of cleaning.

WOK A good Chinese wok is useful if you are a 'cheffy' type person. You can use a wok to seal and cook a naturally curved rack of lamb and other similarly shaped cuts of meat evenly. Just to state the obvious, a curved wok will get more heat to a larger area of meat on a curved rack of lamb than a flat skillet.

MIXING BOWLS Always choose one larger than you require. Basing your choice on thirds is a good idea: one-third mix against two-thirds empty space, thus allowing room to turn and mix your ingredients without spilling. This saves you both time and the frustration of losing any mixture to the floor and to the mercy of your faithful dog. (A dog, he has a dog near food, I hear you say! Yes, even the dog can be a handy tool for cleaning up any mess that may hit the floor, this avoids you picking it up and putting it back in with the mix, for that is far worse. This reminds me to say; African tribes women don't have the luxury of disposable nappies, they are far more inventive when it comes to cleaning their baby's bottom. You see water is scarce in these regions, so mum places the baby over her knee and pours goats milk into the crack of the baby's bottom and then whistles the family dog to come over and feed on the goat's milk thus leaving baby nice and clean. Why am I telling you this? Well, I'm trying to say, we are more fortunate than some other people in this world, so let's make do with what you've got around you and improvise where necessary, now let's move on!) By the way, I also apply this rule when selecting cooking pans.

ROLLING PIN I find wooden ones are the best (and they have other uses, as my wife demonstrates).

All the items discussed above are useful, however, as mentioned earlier, they are not essential; you will find that you can adapt and use whatever you have to hand. Those of you who are proficient in some areas of *charcuterie* may already have invested in some top-quality gear. I'm sure and confident you will agree that if you are to continue down this path, buying the best tools you can afford will reward you by helping you to produce the best products.

BUTCHERY

T oday, there are many specialist books, videos and DVDs covering this topic, but I want to give you just one way that will probably be the easiest you will ever be shown. For those of you who are butchery beginners, this method will give you the confidence that you need to venture into what must seem a 'no-go' area – well not any longer! Right then: "Lights! Camera! Action!!"

You now, hopefully, have before you a pig from the abattoir that has been split lengthways, straight down the middle, to give you two halves, plus a bag containing all the offal and maybe some blood.

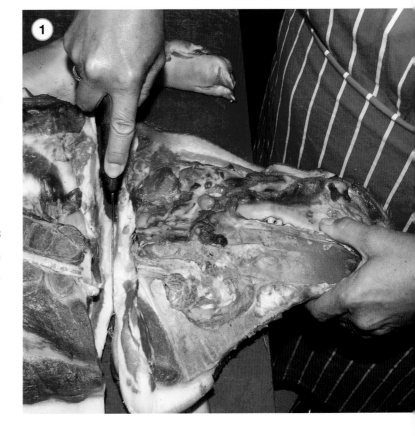

(1) First take the right-hand side of the pig and lay it, skin side down, on a cutting table with the trotters facing towards you. Assuming your cutting table is like a compass make all cuts from North to South after aligning the pig with it's head facing West (that's left).

Now with your boning knife cut the head off and place it to one side – this is now Piece One. (Follow **cut 1** overleaf.)

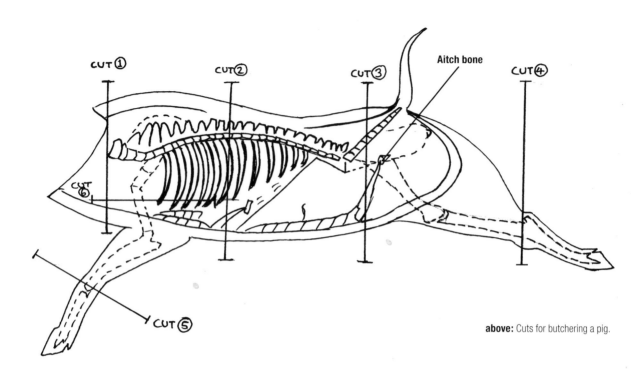

above: Cuts for butchering a pig.

(2) Count five ribs in from the head end, and, using the meat saw, saw square across the chine bone (spine) and ribs. Stop as soon as you feel the bones are no longer resisting the saw and use your steak knife to cut through the remaining flesh – this is now Piece Two. (Follow **cut 2** as illustrated.)

Always scrape away any sawdust made by using your saw; this is good practise and a sign of being a good butcher.

(3) Measure two fingers' width from the aitch bone on the ham, and, using your saw again, cut-square through this bone until its resistance stops, then with the steak knife cut through the flesh. (Follow **cut 3** as illustrated.)

(4) Saw and cut off both trotters (feet). (Follow **cuts 4** and **5** as illustrated.)

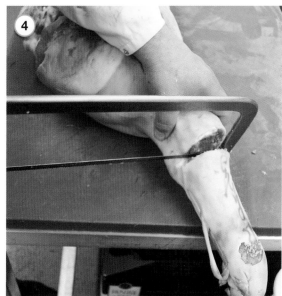

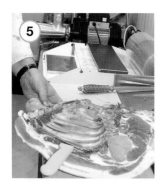

(5) Go back now to Piece Two, the 'shoulder', 'hand' and 'spring' with the first five ribs still attached. Separate the chine bone and the ribs by sawing through the tops of the soft ribs, again stopping once there is no further resistance. Using your boning knife and taking your time, cut out the ribs and then the chine bone. "How?" You ask? Well, at this point it is easier for you to find out for yourself, so go and do it and come back to the book when you are done, having remembered to take your time.

All done? Well done! Easy wasn't it?

Remember this!
It is a blunt knife that will cut you before a sharp knife will.

(6) Now turn Piece Two so that its one flat edge is nearest to you and the hand of the spring is facing North away from you. You can now feel for the ball and socket joint in the middle of the piece and when you have located it, draw a line with your boning knife from the top to the bottom passing through the ball and socket joint area. When you feel satisfied this is an accurate line cut all the way through your piece and the socket joint giving you two halves, one with the hand and the other with the shoulder blade. (Follow **cut 6** as illustrated.)

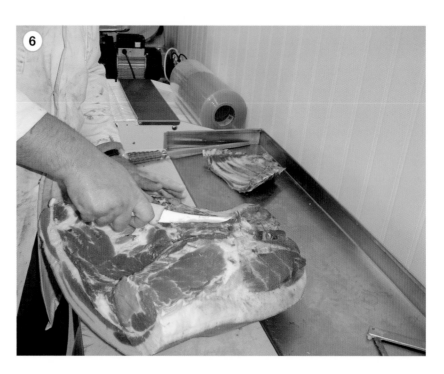

(7) The shoulder blade is difficult to bone out because of its obscure shape, so I suggest you once again do it by discovery for the first time. (You could, if you wish, get hold of a shoulder blade from your local butcher in advance and freeze it until you reach this stage, when you can then get it out of the freezer and cut round the meat using the frozen shoulder blade as a template.) I will say this though, "Don't worry about making a mess of it the first time, in fact it will take three or four attempts for you to become competent." Once you have completed this part you can tie up this joint as a boned and rolled shoulder and cut it into joints sized to suit your needs. If you are going to freeze any of your joints, it is better to score pork rind prior to freezing, but do not score any ham that you may cure. This helps to identify frozen joints in the freezer. Another tip is to use different colours of butchers string specific to the assorted types of meat.

I would use the 'hand' as a joint on which to practise knife skills whilst taking off all the remaining meat. This can be used for sausages or one of the other pork products whose recipes are given later in this book.

Remember this!
It is a blunt knife that will cut you before a sharp knife will.

23

Talking of hands

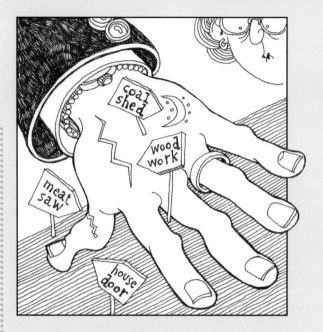

What now seems many years ago when I was living in France, I decided that to utilise my skills I would register as self-employed and open a farm shop with a butchery and delicatessen counter. Starting a new business in France is very difficult and comes with bureaucracy the like you have never seen. The system is so rigid it allows no flexibility for anyone to be entrepreneurial (and that a French word too!). Not to be deterred, I took myself off to the *Chambre de Metier* and asked to be registered. I was asked to produce diplomas to show that I was competent at my trade … but … this I could not do, as my skill is mainly self-taught and augmented over years of stays and visits with other *charcutiers* where we swapped our skills and recipes.

At this point during my visit to the *Chambre de Metier*, I was handed over to a Supervisor who explained that she would ask me questions on my trade and that only if I could answer them well, and if she was fully satisfied with my responses and intention, would I be allowed to register. (I had to do this in addition to attending a week's course to demonstrate my ability, and (strangely) registering with the Service des Veterinaire who act as Environmental Health Inspectors.) I was happy with the arrangement as I considered myself an 'Anorak' on my subject; so the lady immediately started to grill me on the Hazard Analysis and Critical Control Points (HACCPs) relating to the safe handling of foodstuffs. Talk about going straight for the jugular – this woman was obviously proficient at pig sticking as she wasted no time in asking the most difficult questions. All the while the Supervisor was questioning me, she kept staring at my left hand. It slowly dawned on me that she was not looking for a wedding band, but was intrigued by the many scars I carry on that hand. One is like a half moon and shows quite vividly and crudely where several stitches were inserted; I got

this as a child as a result of falling off a coal shed roof after retrieving a football. Another long scar came from an accident with a chisel in a woodwork class at school, and the worst resulted from partially losing my thumb having accidentally put my hand through a door window as the door slammed shut. These scars, along with the single one across the top of my thumb, caused by a slip with my meat saw, were certainly the focus of my questioner's attention.

Finally, the questions stopped and the Supervisor explained that as the daughter of a Parisian Charcutier herself she was impressed with my knowledge and experience in charcuterie and by the work I had done as a *Traiteur* (Outside Caterer). Then whilst still staring at my left hand, she broke into pigeon English and without losing her regional dialect and accent declared: "Monsieur, I think you not good Butcher!" I roared and roared with laughter because I then understood what was going through her mind whilst she was questioning me and staring at my battle-scarred hand! Once I had stopped laughing I did explain how I got my scars, whereupon the lady smiled and duly handed me a stamped letter of authority enabling me to work as a *Boucher–Charcutier–Traiteur*.

⑧ You now have to deal with the middle section of the pig; here you need to take out the tenderloin (*filet mignon*) by first teasing the boning knife under the chine bone and then, slowly but surely, nicking away with the blade until the tenderloin comes away. Once you have the tenderloin away from the carcass, trim and smarten it up ready for use and put the trimmings to one side for mincing.

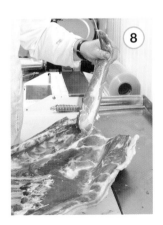

⑨ Again with the middle section, as you did with Piece Two saw through the tops of the ribs, thus separating them from the chine bone. Once completed you can cut out the chine and any remaining smaller bones. At this point you can either leave the ribs on the middle section to cure as bacon ribs, or take them off and cut the meat into boneless chops and belly pork. Whatever you choose to do at this point, this basic butchery lesson is over and you now need to repeat the process using the second half of the pig.

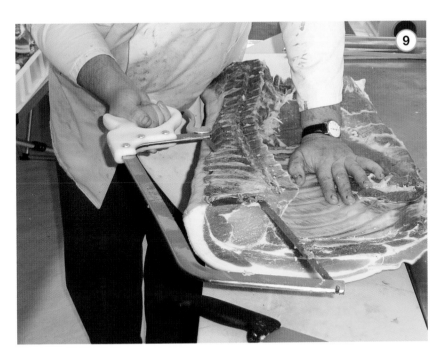

Now wasn't that easy? Starting with this method, you can, given the time and practise, move on to more complex butchery, where you can go further and cut some of the primal joints into smaller and more elaborate pieces.

CHARCUTERIE

"Sharcuter what? I beg your pardon! What the heck does that mean?" These are the words I often hear when I explain what I do for a living. You see, although I am English by birth, (in fact I was born in the district of Swindon, Wiltshire where it was once known as Swine-Down – very appropriate don't – you think?) I am a French registered *Charcutier*, or to be precise a *Boucher–Charcutier–Traiteur*, who practises and teaches this craft here in England. Not surprising really given we probably eat more *charcuterie* than any of our European counterparts, including the French, yet we do not always recognise what it is.

So what is it? Well, it is the artisan skill of taking raw meat and preserving it by curing, smoking, cooking or a combination of all three methods, some examples are; *Jambon, Boudin Noir, Gayettes, Fromage de Tête* and *Pâté en Croute* (translated as ham, black pudding, faggots, brawn, and pork pies) – to name just a few. The trade of the *Charcutier* goes back to Roman times where armies were fed on cured and cooked meats, predominately salamis and hams that were made by the Gauls. You will have heard that an army marches on its stomach; in those times many armies marched on *charcuterie* as it could travel well and did not spoil easily.

Autumn and winter were the favoured times of year for slaughtering pigs as the cold weather helped to keep away any unwanted pests and flies whilst butchering (in fact it was said any month with an "r" in its spelling was good for pig killing). The meat could be eaten fresh during the first few weeks after slaughter, the remainder needed to be stored for many months and only by curing, smoking or cooking could this preservation be achieved. This need for preservation is how *charcuterie*

opposite: Jean Edwards of Deli Farm Charcuterie.

FLASHBACK 3

Are you thinking what I'm thinking?

As a lad hunting with my teenage friends was a regular pastime; we were often out trudging the fields in search of our main quarry – the rabbit; classed as vermin (except on Sunday, when they are classed as game!). With us was my trusty lurcher bitch, Sally, a smooth-coated, black and white greyhound cross border collie. She was classed as HJKC (hunt, jump, kill, and carry) meaning she would use her nose to hunt down any quarry, jump any obstacle encountered in her pursuit, kill her prey with one bite if she managed to catch it, and then carry it back to me no matter how far the chase. She was the envy of all my country friends as she was the top dog in her field (excuse the pun) within a radius of at least 10 miles.

On one such morning, my friends Jonathan and Trevor and I had done the work of three men and caught several rabbits using purse nets and Trevor's jill (female) ferret, Delilah (yes, before you ask, he also had a hob (male) ferret named Samson). We decided to walk home as the rabbits we had caught were in the linings of our jackets and any more would have been too heavy for us to carry. Ahead of us along the river was a cast-iron footbridge where we would often stop to rest and share cigarettes. It was safe for us to smoke there without being seen by any adult as the bridge was hidden on all sides by lush green undergrowth and avenues of willow trees. The ferrets were normally kept in a cloth cash bag tied around the neck with

began. Even though it was the pig that provided the means for men to become skilled in *charcuterie*, the craft was certainly not solely confined to pigs; it frequently encompassed meat from duck, geese, rabbits, game, and other animals of red meat.

I have spent much time abroad, including several years learning my craft in Germany and rural France. In Germany it was enlightening to see the variation in the sausages made after a pig kill; including the famous *Frankfurter*, the *Bratwurst*, and my favourite the small *Nuremburger*. To my surprise the Germans make a delicious *Blutwurst*, which beats all our black puddings for flavour (including the famous Bury Black Pudding) and they also make an excellent *Schmaltz* (pork dripping), sometimes with added bits of smokey bacon. France came next; I trained in the Pyrenees, Limousin and the Charente Maritime. Each region had its own variation of the same type of sausage and each local *Pâté de Campagne* was jealously defended as being the best. In French villages and small towns local people would procure a prepared daily meal from the *Charcutier*, because this would not only save money, but also valuable time – and the meal would be just as good as homemade.

baler twine. This allowed the ferret to curl up comfortably and often fall asleep inside the bag that would then be placed inside the lining of Trevor's coat.

On this particular day while sitting on the bridge sharing 'smokes', we looked up-river and saw heading towards us something that looked just like Trevor's ferret bag bobbing up and down in the water. We laughed and said, "There's yer ferret Trevor, learning to swim"… none of us realising he had dropped the bag and ferret some several hundred yards back. On learning it was indeed Delilah we all panicked, and hurriedly ran over the bridge to the river bank, tearing branches from the willow trees as we went and trying desperately to hook the bag. No luck! There was only one

thing for it – Jonathan was the youngest, smallest and lightest of the three, and with what I can only describe as telepathic messaging – I looked at Trevor, he looked at me, we both grabbed Jonathan, and without a further word we pushed him into the river, right in the path of Delilah!

She was saved and none the worse for her traumatic adventure; she climbed out of her wet bag shook herself off, calmly climbed into a pocket of Trevor's coat, rolled up, and went to sleep. As for Jonathan, much to his annoyance, he not only had to climb out of the river without any assistance from either Trevor or me but he was also denied a hero's welcome! We just laughed at the wet, soggy, dripping mess he was. But he had the last laugh – because he was carrying the fags!

above: 1 Bresaola; **2** Salami; **3** Crepinettes; **4** Toulouse Sausage; **5** Coppa Ham & Salami; **6** Rillettes de Porc
opposite: My first sausage!

So, you have your slaughtered pig and you wonder what to do with it all. Of course, you have your obligatory chops (*cotelette*) and tenderloins (*filet mignons*) for the freezer, or you make some sausage and maybe cure some ham – then what do you do with the rest? Well this book is going to help you find some answers, and boy! are you in for a surprise?

So what makes good *charcuterie*? Patience, a good recipe, but above all – a good pig. I believe that traditionally reared and sometimes-rare breeds are the only pigs to use since they offer all the natural ingredients that a slow-maturing pig develops including fats, antioxidants, and omega-3 oils.

right: The Devon Lop and the Devon Black, both produce excellent meat.

Here in Devon where I live now, I use indigenous breeds: the Devon or British Lop (Britain's rarest pig) and the Devon or Large Black. Devon Lop pigs have their origins in Tavistock where Sir Francis Drake bred them. Tavistock Abbey records back in the 1400s show that swine herders paid for the right of 'pannage' in nearby forests and woodlands where the pigs could forage naturally for beech masts and acorns. Drake may have brought the Black pig to Devon himself; it is my theory that he acquired these pigs during his privateering days when he fought the Spanish and robbed them of their cargos, including their livestock and food that was on board. Drake would have ordered *charcuterie* in the form of salt pork from locals around Plymouth to be stored on his ships for his voyages around the world.

It takes 4 years' apprenticeship and 5 years' full-time experience to become a recognised *Charcutier* in France. This length of time, and the fact that people now preserve meat in freezers are why the art of *charcuterie* is at risk. If you only use one recipe from this book and pass it on to your family and friends, then there is a chance of saving this artisan craft.

By practising this skill, I feel that between us we will also help save the many traditional breeds of pig for which this country is renowned. Commercial breeds cannot offer the same finish to help *charcuterie* as can traditional breeds, so it is our responsibility to choose the right breed for our products. Having done that, we then need to pay attention to how these animals are raised, and more importantly, to the feed we offer them. You see, anyone can give commercial pellets to a pig, but who will go the extra yard to find the natural food that will infuse the meat and fat with delicate tones of flavour? All these factors need consideration, especially if we want to set ourselves apart from the mainstream producers of supermarket products. *Charcuterie* is not just a craft it is a lifestyle!

Charcuterie comes in many forms today, enhanced by the expertise of our modern and talented chefs. Some with many Michelin stars to their credit, these men and women are able to transform meats into plates of sheer wonderment. Now you will be able to follow in their talented footsteps as you begin to discover that the secrets of *charcuterie* are not just for the elite, they belong to everyone. And please remember this:

"Charcuterie – a taste for the future from the past".

As you make your way through this book you may not agree with me, that the recipes are all associated with charcuterie. If you are of this opinion, then I am pleased to know that what I have written has made you think and consider what is, or is not, charcuterie, and I know you are the right person to pass on your individual interpretation.

below: Chef Matthew Downing of the Jack in the Green preparing his cured hams for service.

TRAITEUR

The pronunciation of *Traiteur* sounds so similar to traitor that its translation as Outside Caterer or Banquet Chef may seem unusual, but in France it is your local butcher you call on to organise a buffet or banquet for a party or celebration. It is hard to imagine that in England a butcher would have the skill of a Michelin-star chef, but he could if he were French and had *Traiteur* status. Many hotel or restaurant Head Chefs call upon the services of the local *Charcutier–Traiteur*. If you need verification, check out **www.franckpontais.com** to see what amazing things my French friend and colleague Franck can do.

It's the role of village *Traiteurs* to cook ready-made meals on a daily basis for their discerning clientele, this skill and that of being party chefs when required makes them unique. I'm not going to even try to teach you how to be a *Traiteur* in this book, however, there are a few catering skills that are easy to learn and are in my opinion the greatest fun to execute. Learn them, and I am sure you will be called upon time and again.

One such skill is pig roasting, which has become very popular over the last couple of decades at village fetes, birthday parties, charity events, and as fun food for the evening celebrations of weddings.

So where do you start? With the pig itself of course! It is crucial to choose as lean a pig as you can get, but without sacrificing too much fat, this is quite the opposite of one you would choose for *charcuterie*, the less fat the better for spit roasting but the more the merrier for tasty charcuterie. You see, what happens next depends on how you cook the pig. If you cook it over hot coals, wood, or directly over gas you will undoubtedly

create flares from the dripping fat as it reaches the heat source. My preferred method is to use a stainless steel tray large enough to take a whole pig and one that can be accommodated in an oven (OK, a big oven).

A word of caution, when choosing a cooking method, remember a spit-roast machine can only take a carcass, usually minus the head, and you cannot add any extra meat to the spit. (People tend to ask, "What is it?" when the carcass is headless, thus spoiling the whole meaning of pig roasting as far as I am concerned.) If more guests than originally planned turn up, you will be unable to add any extra meat to feed them from a spit roast, but with the tray system you can add extra joints even at the eleventh hour. Another disadvantage is that it is difficult to carve around all the spit clamps that are used to make a pig 'sit proud' on its mounting.

Another way to cook a pig simply, perhaps at a one-off event, is to place some breezeblocks on the ground in a number eleven formation, about four blocks apart, eight blocks long and two blocks high with some weld-mesh laid over the blocks.

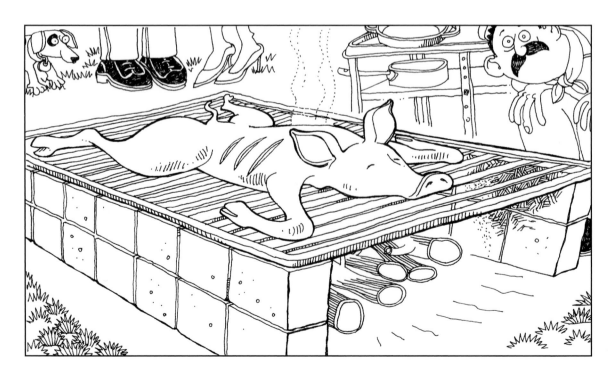

You can place the pig on the weld-mesh to cook over solid fuel. It will take about 7–10hrs, but a butterflied carcass can speed up the cooking time. To butterfly a pig; turn the carcass on its back and saw along and through the chine bone, being careful not to saw through the skin. Once completed, turn your pig over and splay the carcass thus creating a 'butterfly' effect.

Back to my preferred method, the tray system, when I was an active *Traiteur* I commissioned several wet *bain-marie* systems to match the size of my pig trays, so that when my pigs were cooked, I could keep them warm and in excellent moist condition whilst waiting to serve them. Not only that, I had wheels fixed to each leg of the *bain-marie* with brakes and a shelf directly below the water bath to take a set of gas burners used to heat the water in the *bain-marie* above. I even added a tap to the underside of the water bath, so when the pig roast was finished I could use the hot water to wash out the tray on the spot.

I also had a custom-built oven on wheels made to take two pig trays making me totally self-reliant and independent of any outside forces. Each tray could take two pigs side-by-side plus a third butchered and stuffed into the two whole carcasses, making three pigs per tray or a maximum of six pigs per roast. More often than not only one pig was needed for a function, sometimes with a few extra joints if the guest list was larger than expected. This flexible system allowed me to add joints of beef if an alternative was required, I could not have done that on a spit-roast system.

If you start with a tray system, you can ask a friendly baker to cook your pig for you, but do remember to measure the opening of the oven, as it may be a modern deck oven with height restrictions, or one with Dutch barn doors whose width may be of concern. And do allow for heat expansion because you may get your tray into an oven, but find you cannot get it out.

Military manoeuvres

Living and working in Herefordshire after my military career ended kept me in touch with many associates and also allowed me the luxury of being able to employ 'bored housewives' as casual labour. These bored housewives were no ordinary women, they were simply seeking extra income and a means of passing the time whilst their partners, all serving SAS soldiers, were away on official business. Having attended formal engagements in the Warrant Officers' and Officers' Messes, they knew how catering should be done, so they were a great asset to me and required no or little training when we catered at several of the many stately homes in and around Herefordshire. I was never once let down because they all knew each other, and if one could not work for any reason they simply arranged a replacement amongst themselves and just informed me on the day.

Our engagements at these prestigious venues were sometimes on a 'money-no-object budget', so for these functions we could employ extra staff to give us the luxury of working fewer hours. The extra hands would be sometimes the husbands and partners of the female staff. (Yes, that's right, real SAS soldiers dressed up in black and white catering uniform serving people with tiny *vol-au-vents* and *canapés*.) They were excellent at moving in and around the guests and at keeping them entertained with the goodies we had on offer.

These chaps also used the opportunity to have some fun amongst themselves by placing bets on each other to see who could place a tracking or listening device on chosen guests without being detected. The actual 'devices' they used were grapes from the cheese board, green for tracking and black for listening. The chosen male targets were often easy as dinner jackets with pockets could be accessed without trouble, but female targets in strapless ball gowns were really difficult

and proved to be a greater challenge resulting in much fun watching the lads race to be the first to achieve their goal. I often wondered what the guests must of thought on returning home to find grapes amongst their clothing, or maybe some are now raisins!

When we were asked to provide a pig roast with a cold buffet, the soldiers, armed with large steak knives (I'm sure some thought they had a machete in their hands) suitable for carving such a large carcass, would demonstrate their skills (showing off more like!) at sharpening the knives before proceeding to cut up the pig. Meanwhile I would snigger to myself thinking, "If the guests only knew who is carving their meal for them!" One of those occasions was the bi-centennial anniversary of Coca Cola Schweppes™ when the company hired me to cater whilst they celebrated this milestone at their Malvern Water™ production plant in Colwall, Herefordshire. (For those of you who were there on that special day, now you know!)

Another true tale I must tell you is that part of my business was hiring out catering equipment. I had plenty to offer given that I was acquiring new stuff all the time. Hotels, outside caterers and stately homes would often hire, especially during the wedding season. An ex-serviceman who owns one such venue on the outskirts of Hereford, was in fact, an RSM (Regimental Sergeant Major, or in military terms … God!). He had retired from the regiment and had set up a training academy for the supply of highly skilled bodyguards to the rich and famous.

I had decided to sell the equipment-hire side of the business, as I was struggling to juggle all my business needs and I was also keen to move to France. David, the chap who was to buy this part of the business, wanted to come out with me

for the day to meet some of the customers and to talk about the terms of the sale. We had made several deliveries that day when I said to David "This delivery is the last job of the day, so we'll be finished soon". He then started to question me on the performance and terms of the business as I turned the van into a long gravel drive leading to a wonderful large country mansion house. On reaching the house, two BMW cars came hurtling round to the front of the building, braking and skidding to a halt after showering us with displaced gravel. Then masked men bolted from each door of the two cars, and sporting AK47's and 9mm pistols proceeded to fire at us whilst screaming "Get out the van with your hands where we can see them!!" I knew that the rat-a-tat tat – rat-a-tat tat of the firing was only blanks, and that the men were student bodyguards who knew and recognised my van. However, I wasn't expecting this hostage hijack practise and David, who had now had turned a whiter shade of pale, certainly wasn't expecting it! Carrying on our conversation from where we had left off before the shooting, I turned to him and said: "David I think the price I'm asking for the business is a fair one; I really don't want to haggle". David, still white and ghost-like, had a gun barrel only inches away from his face and with his body shaking vigorously he said in a whimpering and shaking voice: "It's OK … I'll pay you the full asking price!"

Back to the pig choice, I should have mentioned that to feed 150 people you need at least a 55kg dead weight, gilt (female) pig. She, like a woman, as we know, will have a bigger arse than a boar and that means you can offer more of the best meat first. Always carve the best meat first, this means starting from the back end and working towards the head. If you get a blood spot, or an area where the carcass requires a little more cooking, it will most likely be behind the shoulder blade, so leaving that area until last will allow the shoulder to carry on cooking in the residual heat of the carcass until you reach it.

above: A butterflied roast pig.

Right, what do you need now for a perfect meal? A folding table, decked out with a nice crisp white linen tablecloth and maybe some Hessian sacking to give it a rustic feel. On the table near the *bain-marie* I suggest a square mobile gas *Bratpfanne*, i.e. a large square German style frying pan with its own burner. Use this to 'sweat' some freshly sliced onions. Wicker baskets of bread rolls for the pork are required; *ciabatta* rolls with their rustic uneven shape are attractive. Finally you will need a bowl of homemade apple sauce and a range of relishes and chutneys. This table should be near the buffet so guests can collect their pork rolls and before moving along to the remainder of the food on offer.

Just stepping back a little, once you have cooked your pig and it is on display in the *bain-marie*, you need to tilt your pig tray so all the juices flow to one end, where you can stir in some stuffing mix to absorb those juices. From there, and before returning the tray to a level position, trans-

FLASHBACK 5

Heavy as a pig!

Ooh! I must tell you this funny story: a few months ago my wife was taken ill and was admitted to our local hospital. While I was visiting her one day, the nurses came to the elderly lady in the next bed who was 93 years of age, hard of hearing and not very mobile. I said she was hard of hearing. Oh never mind! The nurse loudly explained: "We need to weigh you Mrs *Blank*." she replied "Pardon!" This exchange was repeated some 5 or 6 times due to her deafness. I turned my head, glanced at the lady in her bed, and said out loud to the nurse, "51.3kg". The nurses laughed and continued to raise the lady out of bed and into a mobile chair complete with fitted weighing scales. They then weighed her and one nurse, deliberately and slowly, said to the other – "51.3kg". The two nurses looked at me in disbelief, but I just smiled and said, pointing to myself, "Butcher". They said how remarkable my guess was, I explained seeing pigs lain out on a butcher's block offers a great insight to judging weight (*but it was a lucky guess really*). To amuse the nurses, as I eventually left the ward, I muttered the guessed weights of the remaining patients as I walked past their beds, and then – looking one nurse up and down – I gave her weight too! By the way, my wife is much better now.

fer the stuffing to the *Bratpfanne* along with the onions, marry them together and allow to crisp and burn at the edges, which will intensify the flavour of the seasoned stuffing. You are now ready to serve, so take off the crackling only where you are currently carving and do the same as you move along the pig, because if you take off too much crackling at once the pig will lose its temperature very quickly. Using a good quality pair of scissors cut the crackling into bite-sized pieces and serve it on a separate plate. Using a steak knife and a pair of tongs carve the meat from the pig starting with the hams and working your way towards the head and shoulders. It is easier (assuming you are right-handed) to have the pig facing left from you and the hams to the right and nearest to the table. This will allow the meat you carve to fall to your right-hand side, thus allowing a colleague to place slices into a bread roll or straight onto a plate. There! Wasn't that well organised and easy to execute?

The barbecue season can also bring in plenty of work if you are capable of doing it properly. The advice I would give you is "Keep it fresh and simple and use ingredients indigenous to your area as this will make an impact". Back in Herefordshire, for example I would use minute and sirloin steaks from purebred Hereford cattle, and would certainly include local Herefordshire Hop Cheese on my cheese board, together with local artisan-made apple juice from John and Gina Stewart of Munsley who grow Tom Putt apples. When in Gloucestershire I used meat from the wonderful Gloucester cattle and including a Double Gloucester and maybe some Stinking Bishop cheese, which is coated in Perry and made near Ledbury by my old neighbour and friend Charles Martell. It is imperative to have a story on your plate, so let it be a local one.

Putting this kind of effort and more into your business quickly puts the word around that you have a conscience for both the food you work with and the small-scale artisan producers around you. I would get enquiries from as far a field as London and the dividends would pay off in terms of such clients as Coca Cola Schweppes™, Tesco™, Land Rover™, Bulmer's Cider™ and many more. Being good at what I did also brought in strange requests, mainly being asked to cater at weird or strange locations. One such place was a company barbecue for 100 guests on the Severn Bridge; another was a pig roast for the Bulmer family in a graveyard that surrounded a converted church they owned in the middle of the county. Another pig roast booking came from Muslim clients at a school in Worcester. As you can guess, I thought this was a wind-up when it came in until further enquiries revealed that the clients were putting together an Open Day and were offering a pig roast to encourage their English school neighbours and visitors to attend. (What a brave, unexpected and unselfish act that was!)

One county location where we were regularly asked to cater was Eastnor Castle, where we had the privilege of being asked to cater for the odd famous person and many a VIP (albeit all your clients should be treated as VIPs). On one such occasion the castle was hosting the BBC's *Antiques Roadshow* with Michael Aspel at the helm. Michael and his colleagues were to have lunch in the castle dining room, but en route they saw our food display in a marquee erected specially for the event. They discreetly entered and asked for samples, as the display promoting beef from Hereford cattle was too tempting to ignore. Eventually they were dragged away for their lunch in the castle and to meet some of the castle management team. During their lunch they mentioned how much they enjoyed their 'tasters' in the marquee and asked if they could return for more. Well! The castle's Head Chef was furious that we had out-classed him (unintentionally I might add) and that his efforts were not acknowledged, but the castle management were impressed and kept me there for several seasons to come.

The biggest and busiest job I under-took at the castle was for Her Majesty Queen Elizabeth's Golden Jubilee celebrations. I was asked to cater for the castle visitors over that weekend, my remit being to take the pressure off the castle tea rooms, which would no way cope with the expected crowds of 10,000 plus. Everything I served had to be simply made from local produce. Many meetings later it was decided the tea rooms would supply their usual high-class tea and home-made cakes, snacks and light meals, I was to supply local pig roasts, hot dogs with sausages made from Gloucester Old Spot pigs, burgers made from Hereford and Gloucester cattle, and locally dry-cured bacon rolls.

above: Not my stall!! Picture taken at Bath & West Show.

On that weekend we cooked something in the region of 2000 sausages, 3000 burgers and in 6ft diameter paella pans that required six men to lift when full, we cooked several hundred pounds of bacon, not forgetting the 22 pigs each weighing in at 55kg that we cooked, carved and served with too many salads to mention. "Wow!" I hear you say and rightly so, but one word of caution I offer is this, I went from having the country's largest pig-roasting business to nothing overnight. "How?" You are now asking – right? Well, remember Foot and Mouth?

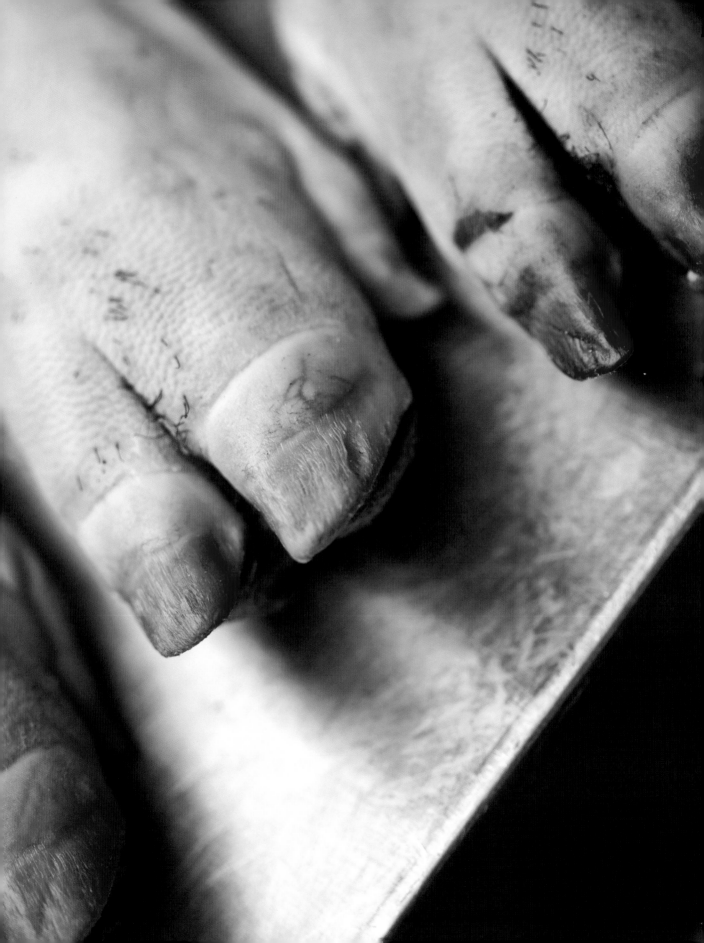

BLOOD

Let's deal with the blood first, as it is the most perishable of all pig parts. You have to make your black puddings rather quickly if you are to use your pig's blood, as it will congeal beyond recovery if left for more than 12 hours. If you notice the blood is coagulating, whisk in a little vinegar and maybe a little salt; this should help prevent coagulation long enough to use. British-style puddings are best in 45mm diameter ox-casings or you may wish to make a French *Boudin Noir* with 36mm boar casings, or a German *Blutwurst* made using the large intestine of a pig (by the way, when I mention casings, I'm referring to the animal intestines that are used as sausage skins). Whatever your choice, you will enjoy the simple process of making these wonderful sausages and whether you eat them as part of a 'Full English' breakfast or on their own with salt and vinegar, they will taste even better because you have made them yourself!

In the *Iliad* Homer mentioned the Greek General Agamemnon who was said to have; "fed his army on blood and onions to keep them strong". This is likely to be true because blood contains iron and protein and onions contain carbohydrates and sugars. The Romans, who were great sausage makers, took the blood and put it into casings along with some seasoning, thus introducing black pudding all over their Empire where each country then developed its own particular type of blood sausage. Thanks to them we now have *Boudin Noir* in France, *Morcilla* in Spain, *Biroldo* in Italy, *Blutwurst* in Germany and *Kashanka* in Poland. Blood sausage recipes don't really work so well or taste as good when made with blood from animals other than pigs: the only exception is duck's blood, which makes a rather nice creamy sausage almost regal in its texture.

TOP TIP

Buy and wear waterproof disposable aprons when filling your casings with the blood mix. I use my wellies and an old rubber apron from my milking days down on the farm so that I can wash them down easily without spoiling my clothes. Also, if you are new to making black pudding, try your first recipe in a terrine before you venture into filling skins. When set the terrines can be sliced and eaten either warm or cold.

A fair catch

I once tried duck blood sausages at the annual Capon Fair, which is always held on the second Sunday in December, in the small village of Blond in the Limousin region of France. This is a great fair and well worth a visit. The village is transformed and the population increases by at least 10,000.

The local fishmonger cleverly closes off part of the village stream to make a pond in which he keeps live fish that you can catch for your own midday meal – a truly unique experience! My 10-year-old son paid €3 for a baited rod and line with which he caught a 2lb trout for our lunch!

With its recent resurgence in popularity black pudding has become commonplace on menus, not only as a starter, but also as an ingredient in many fabulous and varied dishes from black pudding bread, to black pudding hotpot and even black pudding lasagne.

NOTE

Most commercial black pudding makers no longer use fresh blood as part of their ingredients; they use a dry powder mix and add water to replace the fresh blood. I find this difficult to accept and it leaves me with a heavy heart knowing another food tradition is being lost to commercialism. I urge you to seek out the artisan when purchasing such products. Do not be afraid to ask if the blood is fresh or a reconstituted powder substitute before making your choice. Better still, make your own, you know it makes sense!

below: Aunt Freda's black pudding with malt vinegar.

If you do happen to visit Bury Market in Lancashire where the real things can still be found, among the many stalls, I recommend you visit Chadwick's and enjoy a warm ready-to-eat pudding. The stallholders will advise you to simmer your puddings for between 10 and 12mins, but try this simple method that my Aunty Freda taught me and one I have never deserted. Put the already cooked, horseshoe-shaped black beauties into rolling boiling water for 15mins. Regardless of whether the casings split or not, keep at the boil rolling for the full cooking time, just so it's more than a simmer but not quite a full on boil, then with a slotted spoon transfer the pudding from the pan to a plate. Cut and split the casing along the length of the sausage, season with salt and drown in malt vinegar. Absolutely scrumptious!

Black Pudding Basic Recipe

Ingredients

2ltr pig's blood

500g flare fat or cooked head meat

150g diced back fat the best ingredient for
   a British style black pudding (optional)

500g onions

100g pearl barley or crushed oats

Salt and pepper

45mm ox casings approx 1mtr per 2ltr mix

Quatre spices

4 tbsp white pepper

1 tsp ginger

1 tsp nutmeg

¼ tsp ground cloves

Or (the one I prefer) equal parts of:

Black pepper

Nutmeg

Ground cloves

Ginger or cinnamon

Method

1   Melt the flare fat and soften the onions
    without browning them, then put them
    through a blender and return to the fat.

2   Add the salt, pepper, spices, and any other
    flavourings and/or pieces of diced back fat.

3   Whilst ensuring you never bring the mix to
    the boil, add the blood via a sieve to take out
    any last-minute lumps that may have formed.

4   Turn off the heat and fold all your ingredients
    together.

5   Fill the ox casings with a ladle and plastic
    funnel.

6   Let the filled skins rest in a wire basket or
    metal colander whilst you bring a large pan
    of water to the boil.

7   Once the water is boiling reduce the heat
    to 80°C add the puddings and cook for 20–
    30mins, pricking any that float to the surface
    with a needle.

Boudin Noir

This French 'variation' benefits from the addition of 10% cream, apples and/or walnuts. The French village folk are excellent foragers, and in autumn are often seen walking the country lanes with their walking sticks pushing leaves to one side whilst harvesting all sorts of edible treats to add to their black puddings. *Boudin Noir* made with windfall apples and foraged walnuts is a real treat, so when out on an autumnal stroll, think about making your next blood sausage and look for ingredients you can use, or just follow this simple recipe:

Ingredients

3ltr pig's blood
1ltr double cream
500g diced back fat (blanched)
3kg onions (cooked)
1.5kg apples
500g walnuts
80g salt
15g white pepper
6mtr length of 36mm boar casings

Method

Follow the same method as for black puddings.

Boudin Noir &
Chorizo Kebabs

These are simple to make and add a unique twist to any barbecue.

Serves 4
Preparation time 10mins
Cooking time 10mins

Ingredients

Black pudding slices are too large in
    diameter for this kebab, so use;
2 slices *Boudin Noir* per skewer
2 slices *chorizo* per skewer
1 red onion roughly cut to size of meat
1 red pepper roughly cut to size of meat

Method

1 Griddle the 'red' ingredients.
2 Cool and place on a skewer
   alternating with slices of *Boudin Noir*.
3 Brush lightly with olive oil and re-heat
   on the barbecue.

Bolton Bacon Hotpot

with black pudding &
a Lancashire cheese topping

Ingredients

25g beef dripping
8 of 225g naturally cured bacon steaks
2 large red onions (peeled and sliced)
1 tbsp (15ml) freshly chopped sage leaves
1 carrot (diced)
25g plain flour
425ml chicken stock
150ml strong cider
Freshly milled black pepper
150g Real Lancashire Black Pudding® (diced)
900g potatoes (peeled and thinly sliced)
85g Lancashire cheese (crumbled)

Method

1 Pre-heat the oven Gas 5, 375°F / 190°C.
2 Heat the dripping in a large frying pan and quickly brown the bacon steaks for about 2mins each side.
3 Remove the bacon to a large ovenproof casserole and keep warm in a low oven.
4 Fry the onions with the sage in the fat for about 3mins until the onions become transparent, add the carrot and flour, cook for 2mins, slowly add the chicken stock and cider, season well with freshly milled black pepper, stirring all the time and cook for a further 15mins.
5 Remove the bacon steaks from the oven and layer them with the diced black pudding, bacon and sliced potatoes in a deep casserole dish.
6 Pour over the cider and onion stock cover with a tightly fitting lid, and cook in the middle of the oven for 70mins.
7 Remove the lid and cook for a further 20mins to brown the potatoes.
8 Finally, sprinkle with crumbled Lancashire cheese and cook for a further 5mins.
9 Serve with crusty brown bread.

'Full English' anyone?? *(Must be read with a northern accent!)*

When I was a child we could never afford to go away during school holidays other than t'nearby Blackpool for the odd day out, so we would congregate at *me* grandmother's house – quite the coolest place to hang out. There we were with all our cousins (and by heck they were loads of 'em) and many uncles and aunts too, all of whom needed t'be fed. Grandma would count how many people were in house and then send two of me cousins and me to go and buy black pudding, sausage and bacon from Harry Driver's corner shop. She would say, "Ask Mr Driver: Can we have it *in't* book 'til Friday?" as this *wer* payday when all outstanding bills *wer* paid. Harry Driver was a small old man with bowed legs, I think he must have had a severe case of them rickets or polio when he *wer* a lad for he now wore a very long white smock to hide his disability. On our return, just to make sure we had been to the right shop, Grandad asked, "Did *yer* get this from Harry Driver's?" Of course we had, we would not dare go anywhere else! Grandad went on t'say, "Eeh that

Harry Driver, poor bugger, he could never play football nor stop a pig in a ginnel with those legs". (Ginnel = passageway)

Well, the food was being cooked and the girls were toasting bread with long-handled brass forks on the open fire. There was much talk and laughter in the house; Grandma would laugh easily and so much so that on this occasion she *wer* choking with the giggles. She had to leave the house and go into backyard as she *wer* bringing up phlegm, a sight we saw often, *yer* see Grandma *wer* a smoker and would spit on the open fire where her deposits would crackle on hot coal. This time, as the house was full of guests, she went to 'long-drop' toilet situated in the corner o'backyard. Toilets of this type were normal in Lancashire as very few houses had bathrooms or flushing facilities then. This one *wer* a bench-style wooden box with a hole in middle, and a 'drop' of some 6ft to the *watter* below. At *yer* disposal, *wer* shreds of newspaper that *wer* hooked onto a bent nail or, if you were really lucky, those shiny waxy square sheets of San Izal

Strammer Max

My wife, who is German, introduced me to *Strammer Max*, it is made with *Blutwurst* the German blood sausage. Her version of this Black Forest recipe consisted of a slice of *Pumpernickel* bread with a slice of *Schwartzwalder Schinken* (Black Forest Ham) laid on top, followed by slices of cooked *Blutwurst* topped with a freshly fried egg to finish (I must tell you that whilst researching the origins of my wife's recipe I learnt that *strammer max* is also German slang for an erection, I'm glad my name is not Max, can you picture me greeting my wife saying **"Hello darling, Max is here!"**).

Strammer Otto

A variation with the ham replaced by slices of cold roast beef.

*(not that I ever knew which side t'use, the shiny or dull side). T'flush toilet, you had t'return t'kitchen in the house and tip the waste washing-up *watter* down sink where it would fall into a cantilevered 'tipper box'. When there was enough *watter* in the box it would tip over allowing the *watter* to gush in the direction of the long-drop and flush away any solids. As kids sitting on the long drop we used to pretend to be dam buster pilots on a mission, not that we could ever imitate the bouncing bomb effect, but it *wer* fun releasing your 'bombs' to the sound of the long-awaited 'B'dush' and your bombs seemed to take an age to reach the *watter* below.

Grandma, coughing and spluttering, had entered the long-drop to spit and spit she did, but on this occasion out came her false teeth and they went straight down toilet! Well, of course everybody laughed to the point of hysterics, when she came back indoors to tell us, but as things calmed down the question was 'How on earth are we going to get her teeth back?' One of my uncles looked at us young boys and said: "Right then, lets have the smallest lad here then". Thankfully that was not me – I was too broad in the shoulder – it was my smaller cousin Peter. He was taken, (or rather dragged) screaming to the long-drop where he *wer* held by his ankles and dipped down the 'drop' head first to feel for Grandma's teeth. While he searched with his bare hands he complained vigorously about the 'poo down the loo', and demanded to be brought out the hole. Instead he *wer* informed: "Don't be silly lad, they are just black puddings, they won't harm yer!" By heck, it wasn't long after that he shouted: "I have found them!" My uncle Clifford hauled him back to the surface where Peter handed over the dentures to my Grandma. She walked calmly back t'kitchen, where she quickly swilled her teeth under cold-water tap and popped them straight back into her mouth – then she carried on cooking as if now't had happened! I often recall that family gathering when Grandma cooked that 'Full English' with black pudding. Peter was never rewarded for his efforts *yer* know, instead he got a cuffing on back o'head with my uncle balling: "Go and wash your hands, *yer* bloody mucky pup". What gratitude eh?

You can drop the Lancashire accent now!

Lancashire Eggs

Serves 6
Preparation time 20mins
Cooking time 12mins

Ingredients

250g minced pork
250g black pudding (mashed)
6 eggs (hard-boiled)

Method

1 Mix the pork meat with the black pudding and divide into 6 portions.

2 Hard boil the eggs and shell them.

3 Fold the pork and black pudding mix around each egg.

4 Wrap in cling film and simmer in boiling water for approximately 12mins.

5 Serve with a light green salad and herby bread croutons.

Crispy Lancashire Black Pudding Potato Cake
topped with a soft-poached duck egg & tarragon mustard mayonnaise

(Created by Tom Bridge and Robert Owen Brown)

Ingredients

450g Real Lancashire Black Pudding® (skin removed)

225g potatoes (mashed with butter)

1 free-range egg yolk

50g seasoned flour

2 free-range eggs (whisked with a little milk)

100g fresh breadcrumbs

Cooking oil

4 duck eggs (soft-poached)

15ml tarragon (freshly chopped)

15ml mustard seed

15ml English mustard

150ml thick mayonnaise

225g rocket or watercress

Freshly milled black pepper

Method

1 Thoroughly blend together the black pudding, mashed potato and egg yolk.

2 Divide the mixture into four, and with floured hands shape into round cakes, 5cm deep and 15cm in diameter.

3 Dip into the beaten egg mixture, then coat generously with breadcrumbs.

4 Heat the oil in a frying pan and fry the cakes until golden brown on both sides.

5 Keep warm in the oven.

6 Meanwhile, poach the duck eggs and keep warm.

7 Put the tarragon, mustard seed and mustard into a bowl and blend thoroughly with the mayonnaise.

8 Place a little rocket or watercress on each plate, cover with a black pudding potato cake, top with a poached egg and pour over the mayonnaise.

9 Finish with freshly milled black pepper.

Years ago the blood from oxen and other cattle was used to paint the exterior of many thatched cottages in the 'picture-postcard' villages of southern England. Something you should remember if you are on holiday and driving past the red and pink cottages and longhouses in the South West. But consider – today, only the colours are traditional; manmade and carcinogenic chemicals like lead-based paints have for many years replaced the organic by-product – hmmm!

P.S. The World Black Pudding Throwing Championship is held each year at the Royal Oak pub in Ramsbottom, Lancashire. Contestants each have three black puddings to throw under-arm at the Yorkshire puddings placed on a wooden plinth 7mtrs above the ground. The winner is the person who can knock the most Yorkshire puddings off the plinth.

OFFAL

O ffal, lights, pluck, (h)umble or fifth quarter; there are many terms used for the inner organs of animals, but whatever you choose to call them, you are sure to enjoy eating them. We have equally strange terms for the ways we reach the 'innards'; we gut a fish, dress a chicken, draw a pheasant (do I need a pencil?), gralloch a deer and paunch a rabbit.

Faggots (*Gayettes*)

Preparation time 60mins
Cooking time 25–35mins

Ingredients

A complete pluck (heart, lungs, spleen, liver,
 tongue and kidneys)
Belly pork, 25% of the total weight of the pluck
Breadcrumbs 10% of the total weight of the mix
Seasoning: onion, garlic, sage, mace, salt and pepper
Caul fat from one pig

TOP TIP

Cooked faggots can be allowed to cool before placing them in a large Kilner® jar and then cover them in dripping ready to store in the larder until required.

Method

1 Mince the offal and mix together with the breadcrumbs.

2 Season with onion, garlic, sage, mace, salt and pepper.

3 Alternatively use packets of stuffing at a ratio of 60g per kilo of meat to add a new dimension in a range of flavours including the traditional sage and onion.

4 If using a stuffing mix, remember to omit the breadcrumbs from stage one.

5 Layout the caul fat and using a ratchet ice cream scoop (120g portion), place a portion of the mix onto the veil of caul.

6 Cut the caul, wrap the faggots and place them on a baking tray.

7 Bake for 25–35mins at 180°C.

8 If you cannot find enough caul fat, wrap faggots in slices of streaky bacon that will allow the fat in the bacon to baste them as they cook.

9 Serve with mashed potatoes, peas and onion gravy.

(I found faggots wrapped in streaky bacon for the first time whilst visiting a butcher's shop called 'Le Gourmet' near to the town church in Monmouth, Wales. These faggots are probably the best I've ever eaten and I've never quite been able to copy the recipe, so I now kick myself for not asking what the butcher's secret is – not that I expected him to tell me, but you never know.)

Homemade Stuffing

Preparation time 20mins
Cooking time 20–30mins

Ingredients

1 large white loaf
1 onion
300ml vegetable/chicken stock
Sage, thyme and parsley to taste

Method

1 Cut the onion into small pieces.
2 Gently fry in butter until softened.
3 Add the bread and herbs finely chopped.
4 Add the stock and mix well.
5 Roast in a pre-heated oven at 180°C for 20–30mins, or until cooked.
6 For a variation add chopped smoked bacon or chopped *chorizo* sausage to the mix.

Haslet

Originating from Lincolnshire, haslet is made using a faggot recipe with the addition of stale bread at an approximate rate of ½ a large loaf per 2kg of meat. If you are using the stuffing recipe shown then omit the extra bread.

Preparation time 30mins
Cooking time 1hr

Method

1   Having minced and mixed all the ingredients place the mix onto a veil of caul fat.
2   Shape into a meat loaf then wrap in the caul fat.
3   Cook in a pre-heated oven at 180°C for 1hr or until cooked.
4   For additional flavour and texture, place slices of streaky bacon onto your caul fat before adding the mix.

Once upon a time haslet was made in this way but from the now-extinct Lincolnshire pig. This was a strange pig in that it was curly coated and similar to the Hungarian *Mangalitza*, it looked like a pig in sheep's clothing.

Haslet (alternative recipe)

Here is an alternative haslet recipe I used to sell on my *charcuterie* counter, and one that I found more to my taste.

Ingredients

1kg belly pork
2kg pigs' liver
2 pigs' hearts
2 tsp salt
4 tsp white pepper
2 tsp sage
2 eggs
150g breadcrumbs
150ml water
2 cauls

Falsche Hase (False hare)

This is a German meat loaf recipe, which is similar to haslet. For this recipe, I am eternally grateful to two of my friends, Andy and Ingrid Bentham, both of whom were brought up on food scraps including offal. Andy was reared in Yorkshire as part of a large family, which helped him later in life when he became a chef in the British Army. Ingrid knew how to make do with even less than her husband had as a child, for she was one of the youngest survivors of the Holocaust, in fact her food memories take her back to Bergen Belsen Concentration Camp where she spent time as a child along with Anne Frank – no more to be said really except "God bless you both!".

Basic *Falsche Hase* Recipe

Serves 4 to 6
Preparation time 30mins
Cooking time 35–45mins

Ingredients

250g offal minced
250g beef diced
250g pork diced
2 slices white bread
2 eggs
1 onion finely diced
Salt and pepper to taste

Method

1 Put meat, diced onion, eggs, salt and pepper into a large mixing bowl.
2 Cut the white bread into 1cm squares and soak in water for about 2mins.
3 Remove from the water, press out the excess liquid and add to the mixing bowl.
4 Blend all the ingredients until well mixed.
5 Form the mixture into a loaf shape, place on a greased baking tray.
6 Bake in a preheated oven at 175°C for 35–45mins.

TOP TIP

This recipe mixture minus the offal can also be used for German *Frikadellen* (thick cooked burgers) or used in small amounts formed into slightly flattened balls, fried in olive oil for about 3–4mins, transferred to a baking tray and baked in the oven for 15–20mins.

Brawn (*Fromage de tête*)

Another of my deli/*charcuterie* counter items, brawn has been in decline in this country for some years now. The very word 'brawn' and the French translation 'Head cheese' makes people cringe, including those who have never tasted it. I fear this dish may reach books of history and folklore instead of being included as a forerunner in any modern-day cookbook. So, for that reason I will re-name it simply as 'Pork Terrine'. There! That sounds a lot nicer don't you think? (I recall a small country pub restaurant I used to frequent had Spotted Dick on their menu, but were unable to sell more than 6 portions a week until someone suggested they change the name to 'Winnie the Pooh pudding'. From then on they regularly sold 70+ portions a week!)

> **TOP TIP**
>
> A weight placed on top of the terrine will help it to set firmly, which in turn will make slicing easier.

Brawn Recipe

Preparation time 1hr
Cooking time 6hrs

Ingredients

1 pig's head washed and quartered
1 pig's tail
4 trotters
2 Bath chaps (pig cheeks)
2 onions
2 carrots
2 celery stalks
150g parsley chopped
Salt and pepper

Method

1 Before starting, you have the option to pickle the meat for 24hrs. Pickle is a strong brine that will act as a cleanser, it will also dissolve any blood spots and clear away any bone dust that has accumulated.

2 Place all the ingredients in a large stockpot, cover the contents with water and bring to the boil.

3 Spoon off any scum that rises to the surface before turning down the heat to a simmer for between 4 and 6hrs or until the meat is tender enough to fall off the bones.

4 Taking the tongue first, peel off its outer skin.

5 Take off the skin and cooked meat from the head including the ears and chop it finely.

6 Sieve your cooking juice, discard the vegetables and any loose bones, spoon some of the juices onto the meat and season with the chopped parsley and salt and pepper.

7 Place into a terrine to set.

Devilled Kidneys

Preparation time 15mins
Cooking time 15mins

Ingredients

Kidneys (1 per person is plenty)
Dripping for frying
1 'slug' of port or sherry
1 tbsp double cream
Seasoning:
   Paprika, mustard,
   Worcestershire™ sauce,
   Tabasco™ sauce,
   salt and pepper

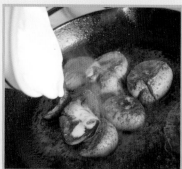

Method

1 Remove any white bits of duct from the kidneys and slice them to your desired size.

2 Brown the kidneys in a skillet in a little dripping.

3 Add a little port or sherry along with paprika, mustard, Worcestershire sauce, Tabasco sauce, salt and pepper.

4 Add double cream and slightly reduce the sauce without splitting the cream.

5 Serve over fried bread, toast or crusty bread, garnished with chopped parsley.

Andouillette

This is a great sausage, adored by the French and yet I personally could not eat one because I think they taste absolutely awful (offal!). They are a true 'Marmite®' product, as with the branded product, you either love them or you hate them. So why do I say they are great? Well, this sausage repulsed so many ex-patriots in France that it made them search for an alternative and that helped my business enormously when I was working there, and for this reason I salute the *Andouillette* and all its makers. Chitterlings or pigs piles are the equivalent to human haemorrhoids; they can be eaten alone, hot or cold or used together with large intestines as casings for *Andouillettes*. The problem being that this is the part of the gut nearest to the anus and without describing in any further detail this is reflected in the taste. That is why I describe it as a Marmite® product; some people have sensitive taste buds and find the sausage repulsive. Even though I have tried the sausage several times and in different towns in the hope I might find a different and likeable variant. Alas! On each occasion sampling this sausage always made me nauseous, so I will not even offer a recipe here! (Mind you, if I were to experiment with the *Andouillette* I would think of including a very strong cheese to mask the other tastes and smells it offers.)

Nduja

Nduja is a soft spreadable version of salami used raw or cooked, I like mine on bruschetta toasted with a little Parmesan cheese melted on top. I also use it in fish soups, Cassoulet and as a paste for crusted lamb and fish for it is so versatile. To make it, I use equal parts in volume of pork, cured back fat and lights (pigs lungs) and mince twice then cure the whole mix with 30g of curing salt (complete with saltpetre) per kilo of mix. Then I bind with olive oil whilst adding minced or finely chopped char-grilled red peppers with hot peppers and adding seasonings of white pepper, paprika, smoked paprika, hot chilli paprika, ground fennel and garlic. Once mixed thoroughly, fill pig middles and tie off and leave to air-dry for at least 2 months, you can if you wish smoke this sausage after the first week of air-drying.

Pâté de Campagne

As the translation suggests this is a pâté 'of the countryside', I suppose we here in Britain would describe it as a farmhouse pâté. It is basically a pork liver pâté usually made to a family recipe and each and every farmhouse recipe will be different. The one I offer you here is one I use regularly as a counter item. It is popular with both guests and clients and can be altered easily depending on the ingredients you may have around or in your larder.

Fills two large oblong terrines
Preparation time 30mins
Cooking time 60–90mins

Ingredients

2kg minced pork
500g back fat
500g pork liver
4 large onions
4 cloves of garlic
2 eggs
150ml white wine
150ml rum
Parsley, thyme, salt and
    pepper to taste

Method

1 Mix all the ingredients together and mince them again, or if you have a bowl chopper, put the ingredients through the chopper until you reach the consistency you prefer. Do remember however, that this recipe is normally chopped coarsely.

2 Place ingredients in a terrine (lined with streaky bacon if you prefer) and leave to rest in the fridge for 24hrs before cooking to allow the seasoning to permeate.

3 Cook at 180°C for 60–90mins in a *bain-marie* or until brown.

4 Once cooled, store at +2°C and serve at room temperature as you would a good wine or cheese.

Coarse Liver Pâté

A firm kitchen table favourite in any household, this particular recipe always seems to disappear rather quickly.

Fills six medium-sized oblong terrines
Preparation time 45mins
Cooking time 60–90mins

Ingredients

4 medium onions
　finely chopped
4 cloves of garlic
　finely chopped
handful of parsley
　finely chopped
4kg pork
2kg liver
6 large eggs
70ml red wine
450ml milk
60g salt
20g sugar

Method

1　Soften and cook the onions in pork dripping along with the garlic.

2　Mince the pork through a 4–6mm plate and the liver through a 8mm plate.

3　Bring the milk to the boil, take off the heat, add the onions, garlic and chopped parsley and infuse for at least 15mins.

4　Mix the seasonings into the pork mince and leave to permeate before adding the eggs one at a time.

5　Add the wine and strain the vegetables out of the milk.

6　Press out all the available juice and add with the milk to the pork. (Alternatively run the vegetables through a blender and add to the mix.)

7　Finally add the minced liver and blend all together before cooking in a pre-heated oven at 180°C until the top is brown.

8　Reduce the heat to 100°C until the internal temperature reaches 76°C. If you do not have a meat thermometer then insert a sharp knife into the centre of the terrine, after a few seconds draw out the knife and if the knife is clean and without any bloody juices seeping from the hole, then the dish is cooked.

Chicken Liver Pâté with Brandy

The perfect starter for you and your guests. Use free-range chicken for the livers and that is the end of my ethical lecture.

Serves 8
Preparation time 20mins
Cooking time 10mins

Ingredients

220g chicken livers
1 medium onion
100g butter
2 tbsp brandy (optional)
Salt, pepper, thyme and garlic to taste

Method

1 Finely chop the onion.
2 Cook with melted butter in a skillet on a medium heat until soft.
3 Add the livers and cook lightly leaving the centres pink.
4 Add the brandy and *flambé* to cook off the alcohol.
5 Season with thyme, garlic, salt and pepper.
6 Place all the ingredients into a food processor and blend until smooth.
7 Pour the pâté into individual ramekins.
8 Cover with clarified butter and garnish with a bay leaf placed slightly to one side of the ramekin with a semi-circle of 5 or 6 juniper berries on the other side.
9 Serve with hot toast.

Pâté de Maison

My homemade version of a plain smooth pâté that can be put together with your favourite house wine, mine being an Australian Shiraz or a South African Roodeburg.

100g per person is adequate
Preparation time 30mins
Cooking time 30–45mins

Ingredients

1kg pig's liver
500g streaky bacon
2 cooking apples
2 onions
½ bottle of red wine
½ tsp thyme
Salt and pepper to taste

Method

1 Cut the liver and onions into small pieces.
2 Place all the ingredients into a stockpot, bring to the boil and simmer the mix for 30mins.
3 Blend the mix a little at a time until a smooth texture is achieved.
4 Pour into moulds and chill.
5 Serve with warm toast and salad.

Up that creek without a paddle!

It was 1976 and the hottest year I have ever known
– if you are my age or older then you will remember
this heat wave as the one that melted the roads.
Down on the farm where I was brought up we had
Friesian milking cows, giving little or no milk due
to the exhausting heat, and approximately 2,500
battery hens whose egg production had fallen to
an almighty low. The cows were lucky, they could
meander down to the river that ran through the
farm and cool off when things got too unbearable,
but the battery hens suffered terribly. We tried
everything we could to keep those birds cool,
leaving all the doors and windows open to allow air
to run through the two poultry sheds, and keeping
all the electric overhead fans switched on 24 hours a
day to circulate the stale air helped a little. We even
separated birds from cages where we thought there
were too many, but despite our gallant efforts many
hens died because of the treacherous heat.

This heat wave also increased the numbers of
vermin we had to cope with, mainly rats that got
into the poultry sheds when the doors and windows
were left open. They would run along the 'poo
trays' where all the hens' excrement fell and from
there they would bite off the hens' toes through
the bottom of the cages, using the dripping blood
as a drink and the toes as food. You see rats are
unable to eat unless they have a drinking source
close by and the heat wave had already dried up
their normal sources. We were then faced with
having to kill our hens for humane reasons, it was
like nothing I have ever experienced before nor do
I want to again, for a teenager this was deep horror!
It's no bloody wonder I champion Hugh Fearnley-
Whittingstall from the comfort of my armchair. I
know from this experience that it will only ever be
free-range animals for me if I were to farm again for
myself. For example, I would want the hens to have
a fair chance of survival if we were to be unlucky

enough to have another heat wave like that one, or
for them to be able to fight back at any rats looking
for an easy meal.

Wednesday was chicken-shed cleaning day
when we would take out the week's accumulated
manure and spread it on the land using a chain-
driven, rear-loading, muck-spreader. Still feeling
traumatised about the loss of so many hens, I found
myself deep in thought instead of concentrating on
what I was doing. In the chicken sheds everything
was done by hand, the battery cages were three
tiers high, 20 cages long and back-to-back, with
three birds to a cage, making 360 birds in each of
the four blocks of cages. The muck from the top
two tiers could be emptied into a wheelbarrow,
which was then taken to the door of the shed
and tipped into the muck spreader (the shed was
built on brick stilts to raise it off the ground, as a
method of vermin control and to compensate for
undulations in the land on which it was built). The
bottom tier was too low for the wheelbarrow, so
we used a plastic fertiliser sack, laid on the floor

and from there we proceeded to scrape the muck onto the sack. It would take two of us to walk the loaded sack to the door, where we would swing it with a: "One, Two and Three!" Then one of us would let go and the other would tip the sack and its contents into the muck spreader. Except that this time, I was not concentrating, and in the confusion I followed the muck out of the door and landed right in the middle of the muck spreader in all that chicken poo!

Of course this provided light relief, just at a time when we needed it most. Everybody was laughing including me. After the laughter calmed down a bit, it was decided that as there was a hosepipe ban, I should jump into the river to wash off the worst of the ordure. So off I marched across the fields to reach the river – in fact everybody took a break and we all went together. At this point I should tell you that there was a sewage treatment works up-river, which occasionally discharged some effluent for reasons unknown. Such practices were normal back then, of course it would not happen with today's strict environmental health laws.

Well, I picked the spot where I was going to jump into the river, a little way down and away from all the picnicking locals who had also gathered to enjoy the river and its waterfall in the shade of nearby trees on what was a terrifically hot day. I wasted no further time, I jumped into the water fully clothed and I can vividly remember that just as I was surfacing, I could hear much screaming and laughter. My head broke through the surface of the water and with my mouth wide open and as I took a sharp intake of breath, I noticed that heading straight for my open mouth was (I will be polite here) something that resembled a ginger sausage and it was certainly NOT the type for eating. You must have seen those T-shirts with the slogan "Same S**T, different day", well, my T-shirt was reading "Same day, different S**T!".

Liver & Bacon

One of the oldest dishes of the last century and yet still a favourite in most households, well among those of a certain age perhaps …

Serves 4 to 6
Preparation time 15mins
Cooking time 30mins

Ingredients

500g liver
2 medium onions
4 slices streaky bacon
Seasoned flour (enough to cover the liver)
50g pork dripping

Method

1 Slice the liver, thinly, coat in seasoned flour and leave to one side whilst you sweat some onions (in pork dripping of course).

2 Add the liver and streaky bacon to the onions and dripping and brown all sides.

3 Make a rich gravy.

4 Pour over and cover the meat with the gravy and simmer for approximately 40mins.

5 Serve with mashed potatoes and peas.

Stuffed Hearts

A dish well worth doing on those grey days of winter after a hard day's work and when you need a 'Bisto® moment!'.

Preparation time 15mins
Cooking time 90mins

Ingredients

Hearts (1 per person)
Sage and onion stuffing (see page 56)

Method

1 Stuff the hearts with a simple sage and onion stuffing.
2 Bake in the oven for 90mins at 180°C.
3 Serve with a deep rich red wine gravy along with basted sweet shallots, mashed potatoes, swede and roasted parsnips.

Offal Broth

Another winter dish that can be eaten from the cooking pot all week long.

Method

1 Dice any offal meat, season and brown with dripping in a skillet.
2 Simmer in a casserole dish along with root vegetables, barley and lentils for several hours, topping up with water when necessary.
3 60mins before serving and only if you wish add some dumplings (see page 182) to the pot and then serve with some farmhouse bread. The older the broth, the better it seems to taste.

Haggis

Possibly the most famous offal recipe of all time and one that is celebrated each year at Hogmanay or New Year to us Sassenachs here in the South. It is reputed to have been invented using the pluck of venison, which sounds feasible, given that there are herds of red deer roaming wild in the highlands of Scotland as they have done for more than a million years. However, today haggis is usually made from sheep offal, that could be lamb, hogget or mutton that differ only in age, size and weight, but lamb plucks are the smallest and the most tender.

Serves 10 to 12
Preparation time 30mins
Cooking time 2hrs

1 lamb pluck
200g pearl barley
200g crushed oats
200g mutton fat
2 large onions
Coriander, ginger, mace,
    salt and pepper to taste
Stock (to cover)

Method

1 Mince and mix all the ingredients together and place into a lamb's pluck casing, or improvise using a pair of tights cut to length (for a large haggis use the gusset).
2 Place the sausage in a pan of stock and bring to the boil.
3 Scrape off any scum, reduce the heat to a simmer and cook for 2hrs.
4 Turn off the heat and serve immediately if required, or when cool, take out the haggis and re-heat as needed.

For a delicious starter spoon some haggis out of the casing into ramekins, top with some malt whisky and a dollop of *crème fraiche*.

TOP TIP

Both faggots and haggis can be cooked in terrines or moulds, so be brave and buck the trend ... cook a traditional recipe in a modern cheffy way.

Hogs Pudding

A pudding with two names, for it is also known as White Pudding, of course like many other products the regional variations of this pudding will depend on where you live.

One recipe is made with offal and groats whilst others are found to be milder in flavour and having been spared the offal, they are all usually made from pork and occasionally veal. One of the last remaining commercial Hogs Pudding producers in the country is Charles Baughan of **www.westawayssausage.com** and he explains that the pudding had its era during the War years. As the ingredients were not rationed, it helped households to have some protein in their diets. He suggests that if you attempt your own pudding you should use ox casings with a 65–70% pork mix along with a cereal binder of either pin-head rusk, oats or barley, adding herbs with salt and pepper to taste, before cooking the pudding in water at 72°C for an hour and then allowing it to cool and dry. You can then reheat the pudding whole or sliced and eat it warm or cold.

FLASHBACK 9

Bottoms up!

Steak and Kidney Pudding is a dish I would choose every time for myself when sent as a child to the local fish and chip shop. I then chose a pudding that is still made today by Hollands® of Baxendale, Accrington, Lancashire. This pâté of tender steak and firm kidney enclosed in suet pastry with lush gravy was my own personal 'banana bread moment'. You see, I would place the pudding upside down on my plate, and smack the foil casing on its bottom to release the pudding. Then I would take my fork and take the top off the bottom leaving a gaping hole that I would fill with malt vinegar. I could then dunk my chips into the lush gravy and then savour every flavour. Can you remember how Graham Kerr the 'Galloping Gourmet' when he had finished cooking a dish would grab a member of the audience to sit down at a well laid table to eat his creation? The lip and mouth movements he made with that reverberating "Hmmm Hmmm" sound would tempt you into wanting the delightful dish he had just cooked. Well, Holland's steak and kidney puddings do the same for me each time I am lucky enough to get one!

Steak & Kidney Pudding

One of my all-time favourites.

Serves 4
Preparation time 60mins
Cooking time 3–4hrs

Ingredients

350g steak
150g kidney
Beef bones
Red wine/port
Marrowbone butter (optional)
Tabasco® sauce
Suet pastry (see page 181)

Method

1   Grease an 18cm pudding basin and line with suet pastry.

2   Make a lid and leave to one side.

3   Dice the steak and kidney, coat in seasoned flour.

4   Slowly brown in a skillet in dripping until evenly browned, remove and keep aside.

5   Oven roast the beef bones in the same skillet.

6   Once the bones are cooked deglaze the skillet with a little red wine or port and reduce, add a little marrowbone butter if you have some to hand to give the gravy a silky finish and a little Tabasco® sauce to 'lift' the flavours.

7   Add the gravy to the steak and kidney, spoon into the suet casing and cover with the lid.

8   Cover the basin and cook in a bain-marie or steamer for 3hr 30mins.

You can now experience a dish where the memories will last you a lifetime.

Los Succulentos Callos de Ca l'Isidre (The Succulent Tripe of *Ca l'Isidre*)

One of my favourite offal cookery writers is Anissa Helou who has skilfully crafted a book entitled *The Fifth Quarter* exclusively on offal. To tempt your taste buds I will end this chapter with a recipe from her book kindly given to me by Anissa **www.anissas.com**. If this, or any of the other offal recipes from this chapter whet your appetite, you will benefit from adding her book to your collection.

Ca l'Isidre started life more than 30 years ago as a simple *tapas* bar in one of Barcelona's poorest quarters *Barri Xino* (now renamed *Raval*, but still pretty seedy). Over the years, Isidre and his wife expanded their bar into an elegant restaurant that is one of King Juan Carlos' favourites. It is also the favourite of many well-heeled Barcelonans, despite its strange location. I was lucky enough to be taken there by a friend who has been a regular since its *tapas* bar days. He arranged for us to have an offal *degustation* or tasting: kid's kidneys, brains, sweetbreads, *escalope de foie de canard* and of course *callos*. This is the best I have had in Spain and here is Isidre's recipe:

Serves 4–6
Cooking time 2–3hrs

Ingredients

6 tablespoons extra virgin olive oil

1 large onion (finely chopped)

1 head garlic (cloves separated and peeled)

1 ham bone

1 *bouquet garni* (thyme and laurel)

150g *jabugo* ham (sliced into thin strips or diced into small cubes)

150g thin *chorizo* (sliced medium-thick)

2 ripe tomatoes (peeled, seeded and finely chopped)

1 or 2 dried chilli peppers (*guindilla*) (crushed fine)

2 tsps Spanish paprika (*pimenton dulce*)

1kg cooked tripe, half honeycomb and half regular (cut into pieces about 4cm square)

2–3 tablespoons flour

100ml white wine

Method

1 Put the olive oil into a large saucepan and place over medium heat.

2 When the oil is hot, add the chopped onion and the garlic and cook, stirring occasionally until golden.

3 Add the ham bone, *bouquet garni*, ham and *chorizo* and *sauté* for another minute or so. Add the tomatoes, chilli pepper and paprika and simmer for 5mins.

4 Add the tripe sprinkled all over with flour.

5 Stir well then add the white wine.

6 Let the mix bubble for a minute or two then add 750ml water.

7 Reduce the heat and simmer for 2–3hrs depending on how low you can get your heat. Stir occasionally, especially towards the end of cooking.

8 The sauce should not reduce so much as thicken.

9 If you feel that the tripe is starting to stick, take it off the heat.

10 Serve very hot with good bread.

11 When the dish cools the sauce will turn to jelly.

12 Reheat over very low heat, adding a little water.

P.S. I've always tried to promote offal to my customers, for I believe if used correctly offal can offer a fine dining experience. One day, one of my regular ladies came into the shop as she did every Friday and asked for Salt Beef in Gravy, which is what she asked for every Friday, I explained I had none left and that she ought to try my Tongue in Cider. I don't know why, but this lady left the shop without buying anything and she was never to return! Hmmm odd that!

FAT

This chapter is probably the most important of all the chapters, because without fat we have no taste, no flavour, no storage medium, no cooking fuel – in fact without fat we would have no *charcuterie*! The best pigs for fat are the traditional and sometimes-rare breeds, such pigs help sustain our wellbeing (however for legal reasons I won't be expanding on that theory). What I will say to those of you who are not convinced that fat is good for you, is that you allow fat to remain throughout the processes of *charcuterie* – including cooking – and only choose to disregard it when it reaches your plate.

In my opinion you should always try to cook meat in its own fat, i.e. dripping for beef, duck fat for duckling, or back fat for pork. Why trim the fat off a piece of meat and then cook it in vegetable oil? I think you get my drift, so go on – change your habits – make the effort to cook meats in their own fat, even if you don't eat the fat itself.

Pig fat comes in various forms:

LEAF or **FLARE FAT** (known as suet on beef cattle), it makes the finest lard when rendered down. Found encompassing the kidneys it is a lining that also protects the pig's other internal organs. Use your hands to peel away the flare fat from the wall of the pig's stomach and then roll it up like a tube, cut it into small 1-inch pieces, then render it down until the pieces, which are called 'skretchings' turn

light brown. In years past, before the age of sweets, these sketchings were given to children as treats, today they are saved for your pet dog! (Sketchings are not to be confused with scratchings, for they are something different, see opposite.)

BACK FAT is the most flavoursome of all and is the best fat to add to sausage, burgers, meat loaves and pork pies. Rendered back fat can be used as lard, however it will not be so pure as the lard made from flare fat.

BARDING and **LARDING** both techniques use back fat, **barding** is the application of sheets or manicured pieces of fat tied to roasting joints, whereas **larding** involves the use of a larding needle to sew strips of fat into such lean meats as venison and hare. The fats then lubricate the meat as it cooks, thus avoiding the joint drying out and spoiling. In France barding is an art form in its own right; *charcutiers* dress their meats, beef in particular, with barding sheets of pork fat. Some of these garnishes of barding fat can look like floral displays, but sadly here in the UK we no longer practice this skill.

CAUL FAT also found in the pig's stomach area, looks like a hair net when spread out and is often used to wrap faggots and French *crepinettes*, it holds all the contents together whilst cooking.

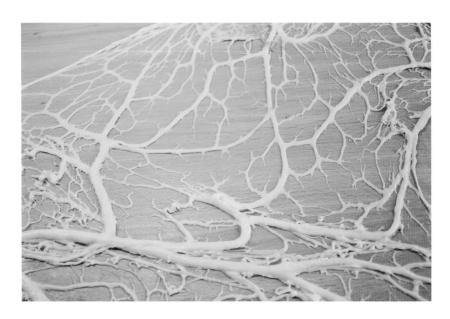

SCRATCHINGS are pieces of back fat that have been rendered out and then cooked at a high temperature to give you crunchy nuggets of a delicious salty pork flavour. Be warned these wonderful snacks can play havoc on your teeth for they can be bite resistant. Scratchings are the remnants of back fat rendering, whereas the skretchings (see page 75) are remnants of the internal flare fat having been rendered.

DRIPPING the term often used to describe the fat secreted by cooking meat. It is particularly tasty and in many countries it is seasoned with salt and spread on bread or toast like butter. Dripping was very popular during the War years. In Germany it is called *Schmaltz* and is often seasoned with bits of smoky bacon that add a new dimension to this delicacy. In Hungary dripping is served spread onto bread with salt and sliced raw onions sprinkled with ground paprika.

The one dish you can't beat is plain old-fashioned fish & chips cooked in dripping! So go on and help change our eating habits and insist that your local fish & chip shop cooks in dripping like they used to.

A favourite of mine is to melt some dripping into a wide coffee cup, then, whilst keeping it hot add slices of chorizo. Mop up the dripping and *chorizo* with pieces of chunky sun-dried tomato bread. This certainly hits a hot spot for me on a cold winter's day!

Whilst I was living in France an elderly lady came into my shop one cold winter's day and asked me if I kept dripping, I replied, "Yes, I do", whereupon she handed me a packet of tissues and said to me "Here you are, you poor thing!".

LARDO is Italian for back fat that has been dry cured and then air-dried, often served as an antipasti, this cured fat is making a come-back in popularity and I fully endorse it along with encouraging you to try some the next time you get an opportunity. Cure for 10 days before air-drying for at least 3 weeks.

TOP TIP

I'll say it here and again in the pork chapter because I think it is so important I have to tell you twice: "You need a ratio of 70% meat to at least 30% fat to make good sausage".

Wiltshire Lardy Cake

A traditional feast best made with freshly rendered lard along with a little salt, flour, sugar, spices, currants and raisins. Bake in a large oval terrine and serve in large pieces. A terrine or closed-bottom dish is important so that the cake can absorb the wonderful juices as it cools.

Serves 8–10
Preparation time 30mins
Cooking time 40mins

Ingredients

450g strong white flour
300ml warm water
150g lard
150g mixed currants and raisins (dried fruit is usually sun-dried in the open air, but there is now a green raisin that is dried in the dark and can be used in this recipe in place of dark raisins)

40g mixed peel (optional)
40g brown sugar
1 tsp dried yeast
1 tsp salt
1 pinch of nutmeg

Method

1   Sieve the flour into a large mixing bowl and add the salt, yeast, sugar and 40g of the lard.
2   Mix together by hand.
3   Add the warm/tepid water and mix thoroughly until a doughy consistency is reached.
4   Place the dough on to a floured surface and kneed for approximately 10mins before returning to the mixing bowl.
5   Allow to rise and double in size – this will take the best part of an hour or more.
6   Turn out the dough onto a work surface and with a rolling pin roll it into a rough oblong.
7   Place a portion of the remaining ingredients onto the dough, fold over in half and repeat the process until all the ingredients are incorporated.
8   Put the dough into the terrine or bowl in which it will be baked, score the top with a knife and then allow it to rise again for 30 to 45mins.
9   Once risen, bake in a pre-heated oven at 180°C for 40mins, or until the cake is golden brown.
10   Once cooked cool in the bowl then cut along the scoring and serve with homemade honey or jam.

P.S. Not what you expected was it? Reading a cake recipe in a book on *charcuterie*. What a delightful way to respect and honour our pig, I can feel a title coming on for a book to cover cakes and other confectionery made from this animal – *To Bake a Pig* perhaps?

HAM

Whether you call it ham, *Jambon* or *Schinken*, where would we be without this cut of meat? The ham is the most majestic of all joints from the pig and the respect it commands is illustrated by the many recipes we have for curing and cooking this king of edible treats, some of which may take as long as 18 months to fully mature. The term 'ham' refers to the rear leg of the pig. Hams can be cut short or long and can also include the trotter. In Spain almost all air-dried hams will indeed include the trotter, whereas in France, Germany and Italy they are usually found without the foot attached. 'Ham' can also mean cured pork meat regardless of which part of the animal it comes from – including gammon and bacon joints – confusing isn't it?

As soon as you apply salt to pork regardless of where on the pig it then becomes ham, gammon or bacon, so to simplify the terminology I describe

it this way; salt applied to the head or forequarter, I call cured head and cured shoulder, salt applied to the middle if whole, I call middle bacon, when it is cut into two then I call them, short-back bacon and streaky bacon. An unsalted leg of pork can be called a ham as I mentioned earlier, however I only call it a ham if salt has been applied and gammons I refer to the ham when it has been divided into smaller joints and slices.

Let us now skip all the jargon and go straight to curing a ham, using one from the pig we butchered earlier (OK, you butchered earlier). There are three types of curing in my book (no pun intended):

WET CURING involves adding the curing ingredients to water to make a brine into which the meat is placed to soak for a set period of time.

DRY CURING my favourite method because it is so therapeutic. Here the curing ingredients are applied directly onto the meat and rubbed into the flesh and skin, like a masseur applying oils to a client, before leaving the meat to cure for a set period of time.

VACUUM CURING a modern method that involves dry curing the meat, then placing it in a vacuum bag and sealing it so that it can retain and use the lost liquid from the osmosis that occurs when the cure mix is applied. This is a very efficient and clean system and one I would recommend you use because it also acts as a secondary wet cure. If you do not have a vacuum packer then put the meat in a plastic bag, squeeze out as much air as you can and then tie the opening to avoid leakage and spoilage.

TOP TIP

When buying molasses, go to your local horse-feed merchants where it is cheapest and sold in large quantities.

Before starting any cure it is important to weigh the ham and jot down how heavy it is. We will assume, for this book, that it weighs 10kg without the trotter. If you intend to slice your finished ham on a meat slicer, then it is at this point you tunnel bone the leg. You can buy a special u-shaped boning knife from your butchery sundries-man to help you with this job.

Basic sweet wet cure mix

Ingredients

1.5kg sea salt
250g brown sugar (omit for a traditional cure)
25g saltpetre
10ltr water
Spices and flavourings

It is worth noting that saltpetre inhibits the growth of *Clostridium botulinum* (a bacterium whose growth generates the botulinum toxin). It also makes the meat pink and firm, so to counter balance the firmness, sugars are added to the cure to enable the meat to relax; but in adding them, remember the meat will become sweeter. You can add spices and flavourings of your choice to the brine; popular ones include juniper berries, peppercorns, cloves, star anise and bay leaves. In the past I have substituted lemonade for the water and Coca-Cola®, apple juice and cider to increase the sweetness and to add flavour to the ham. I once tried Guinness® in place of molasses thinking I could achieve a mild black ham. Yuk, it was absolutely awful! But nothing ventured, nothing gained as they say.

Put your ham into a plastic bucket and pour in the brine until the meat is completely covered. Use a weight to keep the ham totally submerged throughout the curing time. I cure York Ham and *Jambon de Paris* for 4 weeks, but hams that will be used for air-dried products similar to the famous Parma ham need up to 6 weeks.

Some authors suggest heating the brine before use to allow the salts to dissolve before inserting

TOP TIP

It is important to check the legal requirements on the safe use of saltpetre in the country where you are working. It is also worth mentioning that when I include saltpetre in a recipe it is because it has been handed down by several generations in those amounts and it may not comply with current legislation. It would be prudent of me here to mention that I advocate you use commercial cures until you are confident and competent enough to move onto making your own!!

the meat; I must say I often skip doing this stage as I have always managed to get great results without heating the brine, but you will have to test the strength of the brine by either using a brineometer or by placing an egg or potato in the brine to check they float.

The one thing that *must* be avoided at any stage in curing is the use of a metal container because the curing salts will react with the metal and increase the risk of spoiling the meat. Plastic or wooden containers lend themselves best to this craft, however do remember, if you use a large container when wet curing many pieces of ham at the same time, you will not be able to move the container around your walk-in fridge – it will be too heavy! Do also remember to stir the brine from time to time just to make sure that the salts are not lying on the bottom of the container. This can be done whilst turning the hams over every other day to ensure they cure evenly.

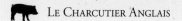
Basic sweet dry cure mix

Ingredients
6kg sea salt
3.8kg brown sugar
200g saltpetre

· ·

Basic traditional dry cure mix

Ingredients
9.8kg sea salt
200g saltpetre

At a ratio of 50g per kilo of meat for the basic sweet dry cure or 30g per kilo of meat for the basic traditional dry cure, add the cure mix to the flesh of the ham and rub it in. Be sure to cover all the parts, including any cavities and only apply 10% of the mix to the skin side. Once you have rubbed the mix into the ham as masterfully as a masseur, put the meat into a plastic or wooden container and leave it in the fridge or a cool place for 48hrs. Hams should then be kept chilled and turned daily for at least a month to enable them to neutralise properly, and to allow the fluids to run off. A note of caution is don't allow your ham whilst curing to get too cold, for if it did then there would be a chance the curing would slow down or even stop until the ham resumed an appropriate temperature.

You can add various spices and herbs to your cure mixes if you wish, but I would only experiment with cures once you have mastered your first attempts at curing ham. If this were your first time, it would be safer to use one of the many commercial cures on the market, as this will ensure success early in your *charcuterie* career. You can move on to designing your own recipes once you understand the chemistry of combining nitrites and nitrates.

For vacuum curing, use the dry cure mix, applied in the same ratio, then seal the ham in a bag and turn it daily for at least a month. If you do not have access to a vacuum packer machine use a good quality bin liner. As osmosis progresses the dry cure effectively becomes a wet cure because the ham sits in the fluids drawn out by the dry curing. In my opinion this is the best of all curing methods and it achieves the most fantastic results.

AIR-DRIED MEATS

For those of you who will attempt making air-dried meats like salami or hams in particular to those that rely on white mould, then this true story is worth reading.

Back in the 1960s a Lancashire dairy-farming family were asked to produce some cheese for their friends and neighbours after they had tried it and had fallen in love with what they had just tasted. For many years the family had made the cheese in the same way in the same building. The popularity of the cheese grew and grew and soon became known throughout the county. It was even recognised by the grand food halls in and around London for its great taste. The family never looked back, and their cheese-making helped to keep them in dairy farming whilst other farmers fell to the wayside.

Fast forward 40 years: the family were outgrowing their little farmyard dairy where the cheese was made. A decision needed to be made as to whether they should expand to meet demand or stay as they had been throughout the years. The local environmental health officers were applying pressure on the family by insisting they brought the standard of the dairy building where the cheese was produced up to date.

After much heartache the family decided to expand, they went to the bank and borrowed heavily. In came the big boys and several months later they had a brand new building fit for purpose – or so they thought. The building, erected just yards from the original dairy, was all-singing and all-dancing; it had stainless steel cheese vats, cheese moulds and state-of-the-art shelving and storage. The floor, walls and ceiling were either coated or lined with washable coverings. This brand new building did not have a single germ in it, nor was it ever likely to if the strict cleaning programme that the local health officers had suggested was followed.

When the day came to move production from the old dairy to the new building it all went without a hitch. Nothing changed, the recipe was the same, the family production team were the same, even the raw ingredients were the same, but now they had larger premises they could increase production.

Several months later when the old cheese stocks were depleted the cheese made in the new building started to reach the shops. All hell let loose and the phone started to ring! "What is wrong with your cheese? It looks the same, it feels the same, it acts the same, but it doesn't taste the same." The comments kept coming but orders dropped off almost to zero and the family were at a loss to discover what was wrong.

The family checked everything again and again and again, but could find nothing wrong. They brought in cheese experts from around the country to try and find the cause but nobody could find the answer. Then one day a chap turned up and said immediately – "This place is too clean, the environment is too sterile!" They went to the old dairy ripped out some organic building materials – pieces of wood and stone – and put it into the new building's cheese store. Months later the organic material had done its job; invisible mould spores from the wood had passed onto the cheese and the cheese started to recover. The family lost almost two business years due to the unforeseen lack of mould spores in their new production. Thankfully, once the spores came back the family were able to recover from their experience.

So, how is this going to help you in your first attempts at air-drying meats? Buy yourself some of your favourite air-dried products and hang them with your own, the good mould from the bought meats will pass to yours. Moulds are competitive, so if you have plenty of good ones available, they will help suppress the growth of the wrong moulds, thus helping you to achieve success.

Consider wooden shelving, because the wood will harbour the mould spores required to aid the air-drying process. If you are going into production in a small way, try asking another producer to store some wooden shelves for you for a few months and then use these as your first points of storage. Alternatively, buy some new rope and soak it in a bucket of water with some starter culture; after a couple of days remove the rope from the bucket and incorporate it into your meat storage area.

TOP TIP

When making salami or air-dried sausage, prick the sausage casings so they can release their moisture; a corn on the cob holder is ideal for the job, especially if it is the type with 3 to 4 needles per holder.

Cooking your first oven roast ham

Method

1 Place the ham on a trivet, an upturned plate, or even a pile of salt, on a baking tray. Any of these options will help to avoid the ham being stuck on the tray.

2 Cover the joint with aluminium foil before cooking, only removing the foil towards the end of the process.

3 Preheat the oven and cook at 180°C for 20mins per pound (450g).

   This is only a guide; cooking time will depend on the size and efficiency of the oven. I rarely cook by guidelines, my instinct is to say:

cook for 2½hrs, then start checking it by inserting a metal skewer to see if the juices run clear or are still a little bloody. If they are bloody then continue to cook until the juices run clear. A meat thermometer should read 71°C near to the bone, but make sure you take readings from different parts of the joint if it is a large one.

4 Given the size of your ham, I would say between 4 and 5hrs will be sufficient overall cooking time!

continued over ...

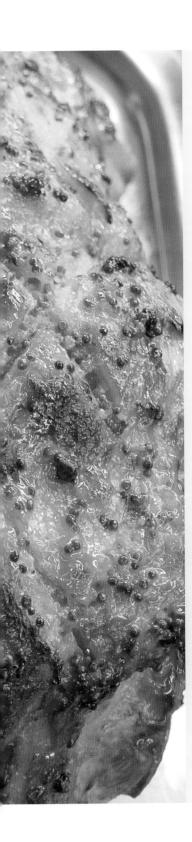

5 Thirty minutes before it is fully cooked, take your ham out of the oven. Then, using two sharp knives already heated in a jug of hot water, cut just under the rind and work your way all around the ham peeling back the rind at the same time, and changing the knife for a hot one as required. Take care to only remove the rind, not the fat, as that must remain attached to the joint.

6 Once the rind has been removed, cut your first line never more than half the depth of fat starting near the right corner and cutting across to the narrow part of the hock. After the first cut make the next about the width of the knife blade (assuming your blade is approximately 25mm wide), and repeat the process right across the ham, taking care to avoid cutting all the way through the fat.

7 Do it all again on the opposite diagonal, thus creating diamonds in the fat. Set a clove in the centre of each diamond, cover the ham with a glaze and return it to the oven for another 20–30mins or until golden brown.

8 For the glaze, brown sugar mixed with pineapple juice and thick honey works well, or try spooning a jar of your favourite marmalade over the joint. Whatever you decide to use as a glaze I'm sure it will taste fantastic.

TOP TIP

Years gone by before meat thermometers existed you could tell if your ham was fully cooked by pulling out the mustard bone from the hock end of your ham, if you were able to do this without much trouble, then that was a clear indication that your ham was fully cooked. You see at the hock end you have two bones, one large and one small, the smaller often called the mustard bone or mustard spoon, for when you pull this out you will see a dimple at the other end of the bone representing a bowl of a spoon. This bone was often used to spread mustard onto your ham, thus having the name mustard spoon. The same bone in reverse could be used on your air-dried hams to carry out a sniff test, ensuring inside your ham was not spoiling. The dimple end was where you placed your thumb and the opposite end was sharpened to a point, here you could pierce your ham in several places and sniff the bone to see if your ham was still OK.

Boiled Ham

1   Place the ham in a large stockpot, cover with either water, stock, cider or apple juice and bring to the boil.

2   Skim away any scum that may rise to the surface and then simmer for the same cooking time as the oven roast recipe. You will need to keep the liquid levels topped up and ensure that the ham is submerged at all times.

3   Toward the end of the cooking time test the ham with a skewer to check it is properly cooked.

4   Once satisfied, return the ham to the pot together with the liquid in which it was cooked, and allow it to cool overnight. This will ensure the ham remains moist, and it will absorb all those important flavours that you have added to the stock or juice in which it was cooked.

5   Once cold remove the ham from the stock and, using the same method as for the roasted ham, take off the rind and then most of the fat.

6   Dress the ham with golden breadcrumbs and place it centre stage on your cold buffet for all to admire.

I prefer my boiled ham boneless so it can be sliced on a meat slicer as required, but I do keep my oven-roasted ham on the bone and have it carved by a uniformed chef using a carving fork and a dimpled ham knife.

Just in case you wish to know why we use a dimpled knife, I'll explain, well having dimples along the length of the blade reduces contact between the sliced meat and the blade, this then allows the slice of meat to fall away from the knife easily.

Air-dried Ham

As we know this type of ham is part of the staple diet of our European neighbours, and as demonstrated by the Parma hams of Italy and the Iberico hams of Spain they do excel at this method of curing. Can we match them? I think not, however I do believe that we can make a perfectly good example if we just follow a few rules:

1: Choose a ham from a traditional breed of pig that has been 'finished' on natural fodder.

2: Carefully choose the curing method and pay attention to the detail of the cure mix ingredients.

The longer the ham is cured, the better the chance of success, so I would start experimenting with a 6-week cure followed by air-drying wrapped in muslin for a minimum of 3 months at a temperature of 12°C and 80% humidity. Keep sampling regularly and note down when you are satisfied with the result, you are aiming for a 30%–40% weight loss. Do remember some Parma hams can take up to 18 months to reach perfection. Most of these hams are from indoor-reared and commercial breeds of pig, but in some regions they are free range and fed on sweet parsnips and milk whey. The mountain Iberian black pigs are usually free-range finished, having been fed beech mast and acorns along with other natural fodder. I think it is fair to say you only get out of something what you put in, which is why the Iberico hams are considered some of the best in the world.

Now you have something to aim for! Is the pressure on?

COPPA HAM offers a clue in its name as to where the meat is obtained from the pig, for Coppa translated from Italian into English means "Nape", so the muscle used for this ham is, yes you are right the neck muscle. You will easily recognise this muscle next time you butcher a shoulder of pork for the muscle is identified by its thick veins of fat running through this tubular shaped muscle. Coppa ham is easily made by following the above basic dry cure method and by adding to the

cure some Italian influence, maybe juniper berries, aniseed, celery salt or fennel seeds. By curing a coppa ham inside a plastic bag for 3 weeks and then letting it air-dry for 3 weeks, you will have a base line to work from to achieve a high quality air-dried ham to your liking. It's simple, if your coppa ham is not firm enough for your liking after 3 weeks of air-drying, then leave it until it is to your liking. Remember you are aiming for between a 30% and 40% weight loss.

CULATELLO HAM is made almost identically as the Parma ham, however the culatello is usually a boned out leg with the slipper joint removed, it is then cured in the same way as a Parma and eventually left to air-dry for around 9 months. It is reputed that HRH Prince Charles is a fan of this particular ham. I will be slated for saying this I'm sure, but I suppose you could call this a quick Parma.

PALMER HAM No it is not a spelling mistake, there really is a Palmer ham, air-dried here in England and in a similar style to the Parma's of Italy. You see, I have a Master Butcher friend called Gerald Palmer who lives in the Forest of Dean in Gloucestershire, where he cures his own hams and names them after himself – much to the annoyance of the Italians! Some years ago Gerald was paid a visit by the local Trading Standards Department who were investigating the claim that Gerald was making air-dried ham and calling it Parma ham. Their enquiries very quickly determined this was not the case and they realised that Gerald was only using his surname for his product, as he is entitled to do. The Trading Standard Officers found the whole affair very amusing, and wished Gerald good luck in his efforts to promote his products on the English market. Gerald has kindly given me this recipe to share with you.

Gerald also makes fine streaky bacon that he models on *Pancetta* and calls it *Palmerchetta* – a truly excellent piece of bacon that I have tried and enjoyed on many occasions.

Palmer Ham

Cure mix proportions (for a 10kg batch)
6.8kg salt
800g saltpetre
2.4kg brown sugar

Method

1 Use the mix at 50g per kilo of meat for a boneless 6–7kg ham and allow it to cure for at least 12 days.

2 Then hang to dry for 3 weeks before pressing it, by placing a heavy weight that will cover as much of the ham as possible on top of it.

3 Coat the fleshy parts of the ham in black pepper to stop any spoilage, and then cover using two layers of muslin cloth.

4 Leave to air-dry for as long as possible, longer drying will improve the flavour.

above: Palmer Ham coming out of cure to be hung and air-dried for up to 2 years.

Black Ham

I was once asked if I could run a *Charcuterie* Introductory Course for a couple who run their own small-holding in South Gloucestershire. Colin and Pauline Dixon who run **www.severnviewfarm.co.uk** had invited several of their friends and neighbours to join them on their farm to discover *charcuterie*. Often when I find myself at these events, I'm asked to sample wares that people have made themselves. I frequently find them unpalatable, but on this occasion Colin produced a fine black ham that looked as if it had come straight from the Black Forest in Germany. I was dying to try it, so out came a sharp knife and Bingo!! What a glorious taste this ham had, "Creamy" was the word I remember using to describe it to Colin, almost as if you could taste the froth from the stout. I was so impressed that I asked Colin would he mind sharing his recipe, and here it is:

Colin Dixon's Black Ham

This is a recipe for a pork leg/leg joint of between 1.5–3kg and about 1.5–2kg salt in all – for larger joints increase the ingredients accordingly.

Method

1   Stab the rind of the pork all over with a very sharp thin knife to allow the salt to penetrate the skin.

2   Rub the joint all over with fine sea salt – rubbing well into the flesh and the rind, remember you can use coarse sea salt by first pounding it in a pestle and mortar to the consistency required.

3   In a non-metallic bowl/tub cover the bottom with about ½ inch of sea salt and place the pork onto it.

4   Cover the pork with salt ensuring it is well covered. It does not need to be immersed in salt, just covered with a layer.

5   Leave for 7 days, turning daily and making sure that it stays covered with salt.

6   Remove the joint from the salt, wash thoroughly and then dry.

7   Make up a pickle brine with the following ingredients:

1ltr dark beer or stout	225g sea salt
225g treacle or molasses	1 tbsp juniper berries
225g soft brown sugar/muscavado	1 tbsp black peppercorns

8   Heat the ingredients together until all the sugar and salt is fully dissolved, then allow to cool.

9   Immerse the pork in the pickle ensuring that all of it is completely covered – top up with water or beer (no more than 0.5ltr water) to cover the joint.

10   Weight the joint down to ensure it does not float to the surface.

11   Leave in the pickle for 6 weeks, turning weekly.

12   Take the joint out of the pickle, wash thoroughly and dry.

13   Wrap in a muslin cloth.

14   Dry the ham in a cool airy (draughty) place for 4 weeks.

15   This ham can then be cold smoked for 3–4 days.

BACON

Ham is also known as bacon and comes in several forms: smoked, black and green, all of which can be produced in such cuts as Ayrshire, middle, collar, streaky and short-back bacons to name but a few.

SMOKED BACON – exactly what it says on the packet, i.e. bacon that has been smoked, usually after curing. There are many forms of smoking, you can brush-wash your bacon with a liquid smoke, or you can give it a smoked flavour by using dry powder added to the cure mix. I still stick to the authentic traditional method of cold smoking for added flavour and longevity, because smoking in the traditional way can extend the life of sliced bacon by 4 weeks or more. It is better to use dry-cured bacon for smoking as wet-cured meats don't allow the smoke to take hold properly and can spoil the meat by turning it rancid. Green sliced pre-packed bacon would normally have a 6-week shelf life, however if it were smoked, its product life could be increased to 10 weeks.

BLACK BACON – can be achieved by adding molasses to your wet cure. This gives the bacon a very distinctive look and mature flavour, one that is aesthetically pleasing to the generation of folk who grew up in such counties such as Shropshire, Suffolk and Devon where this traditional fayre was commonplace. The best black bacon I have experienced was *Schwartzwalder Schinken*, loosely translated as 'bacon from the Black Forest' in Germany – I must return there one day to acquire an original recipe.

GREEN BACON – the term given to what we know as un-smoked bacon. Occasionally you can see a green tinge on this bacon's surface, rather like a thin film of oil lying on water. This is perfectly harmless and is probably how green bacon got its name, it is the result of a chemical reaction during the curing.

AYRSHIRE BACON – made from the middle part of a pig. It is usually wet cured, without any bones attached, often rindless and rolled and tied with the loin in the middle of the roll. Ayrshire is a large Scottish county

TOP TIP

Bacon bits and odd shapes left over from your bacon slicer can be saved and used in a pea soup or minced and added to pork pie ingredients.

where Ayrshire cattle frequent lush grasslands. Their milk was often fed to pigs kept in large rearing units alongside the dairies. Without a doubt, in my opinion, pigs fed on milk will produce the most delicious pork you could ever ask for.

MIDDLE BACON – also uses a whole pig middle, that is either dry or wet cured and then folded flat in half by bringing the streaky over to the edge of the loin. If you leave the ribs on the flitch whilst curing and then take them off as a sheet you will have bacon ribs that can be boiled and eaten with mushy peas – one of my favourite meals.

FLASHBACK 10

Does 1lb = £1.00?

As a lad, I had to do most of the family shopping with my two sisters because many pairs of hands were needed to carry the heavy bags. We would be sent to specific shops in our local neighbourhood, for example, the double-fronted greengrocer on Able Street for the freshest green produce. For the fruit we would walk to another greengrocer some half a mile away who sold what was called 'cut-fruit,' i.e. fruit that was on the turn and sold for less than half price after the shopkeeper had cut out any bruises. He also sold 'pet food'; these were vegetables that were past their prime and sold off to feed rabbits and guinea pigs (we ate a lot of 'rabbit vegetables' even though we only ever had a dog). Two butchers were on our list: Mr Ingham for sausage and pork joints and Mr Loftus for anything other than pork. I do remember that when we were really poor and had nothing in the larder, Dad would send us kids to Mr Loftus to ask for bacon ribs, which in those days were given away as a by-product. Bacon ribs are still one of my favourite food items today and bring back fond memories of eating with my family as a child. Now I am old enough to understand these economies, I am very proud of where I came from and this must be a credit to all those people around me at that time in my life.

I also remember as a very young lad being sent to Mr Ingham for 1lb of his best sausage. Mr Ingham was a heavy man with rosy red cheeks, probably the result of working in a chilled environment all day, or perhaps he was a heavy drinker as were most men in Lancashire at that time? I gave Mr Ingham a £1 note for the sausage and was about to leave when he shouted "WAIT!" He then came round from his counter, leaned over to me, and pressed some change in my hand saying with a wink, "Go straight home lad and give your mother the money". I thought the sausage cost £1 as I had asked for a 1lb of sausage! This left me very confused and I cried all the way home, sometimes stopping to throw the sausages to the ground in order to hurt, bruise, or hopefully burst them, as I thought my mother and the butcher were maybe doing things that allowed us to have cheap meat!! I can laugh now when I think of my naivety in those early childhood days.

Bacon Ribs & Mushy Peas

Having acquired a sheet of cured bacon ribs, cut them into pairs, put them in a large stockpot and cover them with water. Bring the water to the boil, and skim off any scum that rises to the surface using a slotted spoon.

Turn down the heat and simmer for approximately 2hrs or until the meat starts to fall off the bone. Serve in a pile in the middle of your kitchen table along with a dish of mushy peas as a dip. Just watch everybody fight over the ribs as they become fewer! (Dad, I always remember you when I make or eat this recipe.)

COLLAR BACON – made from the shoulder this cut offers a broader slice with more fat than those above. It is seldom heard of today, much to my dismay.

SHORT-BACK and **STREAKY BACON** – are the result of cutting the middle bacon into two sides. Short-back bacon is also called **loin** bacon and streaky is often referred to as **belly** or **breakfast bacon**; the air-dried Italian equivalent is known as *Pancetta*.

TOP TIP

When *pancetta* is cooked to a crispy finish without being too brittle, the top third can be dipped into melted chocolate orange and used as a garnish in desserts, also cooked micro lardons covered in chocolate make a most refreshing change as a dressing to a light citrus salad or even a chilled mixed fruit dessert.

Roll up! Roll up!

Whilst living in France I came across Bacon Roly Poly for the first time. I was visiting the Limousin region looking for authentic French recipes when I met an English gypsy traveller who showed and cooked this recipe for my wife and me. He opened a packet of ready-made shortcrust pastry from a local supermarket and rolled it out, and then he placed bacon, sliced onion and sage onto the pastry and proceeded to roll it up as you would a Swiss Roll. Having tied it up in the pastry's original greaseproof paper and then a chequered tea towel, he put it into a cast-iron cooking pot, covered it with water and cooked it over an open fire for 2hrs.

Whilst waiting for our treat, Del our gypsy traveller went on to tell us about other culinary treats he had eaten by the roadside as a child, often with his grandmother. These recipes included squirrel and hedgehog baked in clay complete with entrails, "Out of choice?" I asked "No, out of bloody necessity" he replied. He also shared how he and his grandmother picked herbs from the hedgerows to brighten up a meal and how they stole pigs' trotters from a village butcher in order to make a stew. He described this as an 'honourable' theft by saying they left all the expensive steaks behind, so as not to bring bad luck to the butcher's trade. (*I drew the line here with my humour, for I had Del the gypsy wheeler-dealer who spoke in cockney rhyming slang and trotters as a main ingredient for a joke or one liner, I just bit my lip and enjoyed the stories told and recipes he shared.*)

Even though I was in France to find French recipes, I could not hide my delight at this simple but delicious treat. If I were to change anything about this wonderful recipe it would be to use suet pastry in lieu of the shortcrust. Thanks Del, I enjoyed all your stories!

LARDONS OF BACON – can easily be made by slicing streaky bacon approximately 1cm thick and then cutting the slices into 1cm cubes.

Lardon, Gesier & Citrus Salad

Method

1 Arrange a salad of your choice (I like citrus fruits along with a few crushed walnuts).
2 Toss in a dressing and arrange on your plate.
3 Sauté some lardons and chicken gizzards (*gesiers*) in a skillet whilst putting your salad together.
4 Spoon the warm lardons and *gesiers* over the salad and serve immediately.
5 A fresh warm piece of puff pastry is a great accompaniment to this salad.

KASSLER – the German version of cured loin (eye of loin) of pork. It is often served with *sauerkraut*.

BATH CHAPS – back in fashion I am pleased to say. For those of you who are not sure what they are, I will describe them. A pig has a face with two cheeks, these cheeks complete with their surrounding fatty tissue are cut away from the head and placed in brine for 3–5 days, after which the 'chaps' are cooked in stock and allowed to cool before slicing. This was often the ham that household servants ate at picnics whilst the gentry ate the more-expensive cuts. Pigs cheeks are strictly speaking the fleshy muscle part of the chap and when cured along with the fatty surround it then becomes the Bath Chap.

Jambon de Persille
(Ham & Parsley)

Have you ever wondered what to do with those ham hocks? Try this recipe; it is so easy you will wonder why you don't sell them at your local farmers' market!

Method

1 Julienne some cooked ham and then cut again against the length into tiny cubes (*mirepoix*).

2 Add sliced baby *cornichons* (gherkins) and coarsely chopped parsley.

3 Mix together and either spoon into *verrines* (glass beakers) or into a terrine.

4 Make some gelatine from trotters and leftover bones.

5 Flavour with stock (or cheat – use a stock cube and powdered gelatine).

6 Add in some optional brandy, port or Madeira (about 2–3 tablespoons) and spoon over the *Jambon* mix.

7 No other seasoning is required as enough flavour comes through from the ham and the pickled *cornichon*.

8 Place your terrine / *verrines* in the fridge to set.

9 Serve as a starter, ideally with a light salad and country bread.

Jambon de Pâques
(Easter Ham)

The same as the recipe opposite, except that hard-boiled quail eggs are peeled and placed in the centre of each mix in the *verrines*, or hens' eggs are placed in the terrine end-to-end in the middle of the mix as for a Gala Pie (see page 146). If you 'top and tail' the eggs until the yolk can be seen, the egg whites and yolks will be visible in every slice.

Lincolnshire Chine

Unique to this wonderful county, but a great alternative to display on a cold meats counter anywhere. To make it, you need a complete forward section of the pig. Saw either side of the chine bone leaving a joint approximately 150–170mm wide that should be wet cured for 14 days. After the cure place the joint on its side and with a sharp knife draw the blade from the back fat to the chine bone creating 1cm slices right along the joint. Do this until you have completed the cuts in a sandwich effect.

Now fill the cuts with herbs, wrap the joint in a cooking bag and slow cook it in stock for 2½–3hrs, then allow it to chill before slicing thinly to serve. You could at this stage take the meat off the bone in order to slice on an automated slicer. The contrast between strips of pink ham and green herbs really make an eye-catching product.

Pea & Ham Soup

A dish so simple I'm almost embarrassed by telling you how to put it together.

Ingredients

1 packet dried peas
Cooked bacon and/or leftover ham pieces

Method

1 Empty a packet of dried peas into a basin, cover with water and add the bi-carbonate of soda tablet that was included in the packet.
2 Leave to soak overnight.
3 Next day change the water and add cooked bacon or ham bits to the peas.
4 Without bringing it to the boil, warm the mix through until the peas are cooked.
5 Serve with chunky bread and butter.

If you prefer a smooth pea soup, blend the pea mix with some extra water and add a little cream for sophistication before adding your bacon bits. You may wish to check the soup for seasoning, however the salt from the bacon is usually adequate.

Pea & Ham Verrine

A great starter dish worth all the effort it requires, particularly if you have guests who will marvel at your expertise. This dish is made with every British ham classic you can think of, it has ham and melon, ham and mustard, potted ham, pea and ham, ham and tomato, bacon and egg and last but not least, it is also a BLT if you consider the rocket as lettuce. It sounds busy with all those ingredients but believe me it really works!

Method

1. Shred some ham from a cooked hock.
2. Add cooked garden peas and mustard seeds for colour and warmth.
3. Fold together and fill one third of a glass.
4. Use 4 leaves of gelatine to 0.5ltr of watermelon juice to make a *jus*.
5. Pour the *jus* over the meat and leave to set for about 40mins.
6. Once set, add round discs of black ham (cut from slices with a pastry cutter), melon balls and baby tomatoes, more black ham with a topping of crunchy streaky bacon bits, chopped boiled egg and micro leaves of wild rocket to garnish.

This is Michelin Star food, so go on, give it a go!

I created this dish and entered it in ITV's *Britain's Best Dish* television competition. I'm pleased to say I did rather well with it, eventually losing out in the Regional Final, but not before the judges said that they felt that my dish and the winning dish were probably the best two in the whole competition! Ever since hearing those comments I've felt a winner – and all the more determined to pass on my knowledge for others to share. I'm sure that given time my view will change to, "What if I had won?" and "What would I have done with the £10,000 prize-money?" but in the meantime I'll settle for a Cheshire cat smile.

I once tried *Dachs Schinken* (badger ham) in Germany and at the time I was given this air-dried meat to taste, I had no idea from which animal it came, I just had to guess what it was by tasting. I tried in vain to guess correctly and had suggested wild boar and even pot-bellied pig, but alas I needed more clues. Once I learned the animal's size and that its fur was black and white the penny (or Deutsch Mark as it was then) dropped, it really was badger. A surprise indeed! I avoided asking any questions as to how it met its death (maybe that was my first road kill), I just complimented the men who asked me to taste it and strolled on, hearing fits of laughter behind me as I went.

Croque-monsieur

A toasted ham and cheese sandwich that originated in France where it is often made using Emmental or Guryere cheese. A *béchamel* sauce is sometimes served with this dish in restaurants.

Croque-madame

The same as monsieur, but with a fried egg on top (I'm not going to tell you what the egg represents!).

Monte Cristo

A ham and cheese sandwich, which is coated in batter and then deep fat fried (in pork dripping I hope).

3BBBs

Better known as a bacon and brie baguette this is a simple but yummy sandwich made from a freshly made crunchy baguette filled with hot bacon and thin slivers of a brie that partly melts when it meets the hot bacon. The addition of a little redcurrant jelly offers a new dimension to this sandwich.

BLT

Deserves to be mentioned here, because there are still some people who may not know this sandwich by its full name. The bacon, lettuce and tomato sandwich has become famous through the generations of clerical workers who look for a light lunch but are still hanging on to their lust for the bacon they probably swapped for a bowl of healthy muesli at breakfast time.

Devils on Horseback

A strange name for this *canapé* of streaky bacon wrapped around a large pitted prune. Bake in the oven and serve either warm or cold.

Angels on Horseback

Made with oysters treated in the same way as prune 'devils'.

Egg & Bacon Flan (*Quiche Lorraine*)

Whatever you want to call this dish, it will certainly delight those who are lucky enough to devour a warm slice.

Serves 8
Preparation time 20mins
Cooking time 50mins including the blind baking

Ingredients

Short-crust pastry (see page 180)
2 medium onions
2 tomatoes (sliced) (optional)
200g smoked bacon
5 eggs
0.5ltr full-fat milk
200g cheese (grated)

Method

1 Grease and line a false-bottomed flan tin with short-crust pastry.

2 Bake blind at 200°C for 12mins.

3 Meanwhile gently *sauté* some onions with some smoked bacon bits to place on the pastry when it is ready.

4 Mix eggs and milk together, season with salt and pepper.

5 Beat well, and pour into the pastry case.

6 Scatter over the filling with grated cheese.

7 Add some sliced tomato to the surface before cooking to offer a little colour to the finished flan (optional).

8 Place in an oven preheated to 180°C and bake for 30 to 40mins or until golden brown.

Ham & Pineapple Pizza

Serves 8–10
Preparation time 30mins
Cooking time 20–30mins

Ingredients

Pizza dough
2 red onions (sliced)
2 cloves of garlic (crushed into a paste)
50g ham
150g pineapple chunks (tinned or fresh)
4 tbsp tomato sauce
120g cheese (grated)

Method

1 Roll pastry dough into a circle.
2 Spread with a tomato sauce and garlic paste.
3 Add sliced red onions.
4 Tear ham and scatter over the pizza along with pineapple chunks.
5 Grate cheese over the top.
6 Place in an oven preheated to 180°C and bake for 25mins or until the dough is crisp and until the cheese has all melted.

Q: Waiter, waiter, will my pizza be long?

A: No Sir! It will be flat and round.

From the sublime to the ridiculous

It was February and I had just visited a *Fête du Cochon* (pig festival) in the small French mountain town of St Pons way up in the Pyrenees. A festival, which if carried out in the same way in England, would have been closed down immediately by all the do-gooders, animal activists and local authorities. You see it was a pig-killing demonstration right in the middle of the town square. This was followed by butchery lessons and then all the women set about cooking the meat in large cauldrons fuelled by vine cuttings from the nearby vineyards. The meat was served along with producing *boudin noir* and pork sausages, which were all made on the day and then eaten by the many hundreds of visitors who had travelled to this mediaeval town.

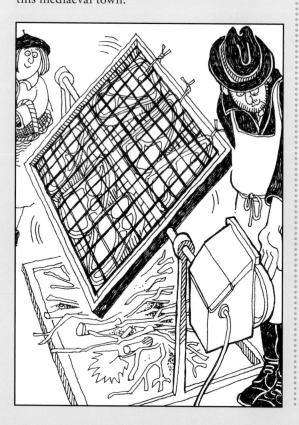

I saw for the first time whilst in St Pons a novel, homemade spit-roasting machine. It was driven by a cement mixer with the drum removed; a shaft about 5–6ft long had been inserted into the drive of the mixer with its opposite end resting on an axle stand of some kind. Welded to the shaft were two flat, square weld mesh baskets positioned at right angles to ease the revolving shaft when fully laden. The baskets were in the same style as those enveloped wire racks use for barbecuing fish, but larger versions of course. The baskets were loaded with hams of pork and cooked over a fire of vine trimmings before being carved up later that same evening for sale to the public.

Driving through France on my return home from St Pons allowed me to visit many other towns on and off my route and one such place was the small village of Roquefort-sur-Soulzon where the famous blue cheese is made. As you drive towards this hilly village, you see fields full of the very sheep whose milk that goes into making this exquisite cheese. The lactation period for these sheep is less than 6 months, which is why the cheese sells out quickly each year.

There are many companies making cheese in the village and some offer tours around the caves in which they are stored. I joined one of these tours and was mighty surprised and impressed by the story and history attached to this world-renowned product. In the caves themselves I was awestruck at the number of round wheels of cheese stored to mature in the dark cool cavern, protected behind a shield of glass. "Wow! Look at those cheese, there must be thousands," I said to my wife, just then the tour guide broke into English and said in her unmistakable French accent "Ah oui Monsieur, it is a tragedy is it not?". "A tragedy Madame?" I asked. "Oui, Monsieur, the cheese they are all plass-teak!"

Pig in a Blanket

"Pig in a blanket" means different things in different parts of the country, this version is from Ledbury in Herefordshire. It is a great savoury made easily with a 5-inch square piece of puff pastry (see page 180). Roll the pastry out in front of you, cut it into a diamond and assuming the corners are points of a compass, place a slice of bacon from West to East, cover with tomato slices, a thin plain pork sausage and finally some grated cheese. Now fold the North and South corners together, thus wrapping the contents up nice and snug. Brush lightly with an egg wash, then place in a preheated oven at 180°C and bake until golden brown.

Chicken & Ham Pie

A British classic sometimes made from the Sunday lunch leftovers with a few added leeks. Sweat some onions in butter then add pieces of raw ham and chicken having first coated them in seasoned flour, place all the ingredients in a pie dish lined with short-crust pastry (see page 180) along with some double cream and cover with a short-crust lid. Place in an oven, preheated to 180°C and bake for 1hr or until golden brown.

Full English

A meal for breakfast, but often eaten at any time these days. Usually involves a combination of bacon, sausage, black pudding, mushrooms, toast, baked beans, fried tomato, fried bread, fried egg, hash browns (OK these are American, I know!) and a mug of tea. We all know there are other variations of this meal, but it was worth a mention for the number of *charcuterie* items included in this important dish. When I was in the Army it was an offence to miss taking this meal and you could be charged and jailed if you were to be caught not doing so, because it was known as the 'CO's (commanding officers) Parade'! You see an army does really and truly march on its stomach.

SMOKING

left to right: cold smoked meats;
a traditional hot-smoke kipper house;
a man who takes pride in his work.

I'm going to avoid writing a long chapter on smoking because it can rapidly become very confusing, and as I said earlier in this book, I am not writing about the science and complexities of *charcuterie*, but simply listing my tips for you to consider as you venture into the craft. I am aware that you will have some burning questions that will hopefully be answered as you read on. The tips I offer are designed to fire up your enthusiasm, not only to become successful at smoking your own foodstuffs, but also to build your own smoker in which to do it!

There are two types of smoking to consider, hot and cold. There is smoking to achieve flavour, and smoking to preserve and extend shelf life. In the simplest terms: you can get away with a short smoke if you only want flavoursome meat, but if you wish to preserve your meat then it is essential to smoke it for a lengthy period.

HOT SMOKING

Hot smoking is best carried out between 32°C and 72°C but I rarely hot smoke above 60°C. I do not recommend hot smoking for such large pieces of meat as hams, because they can harden quickly on the outer surface trapping moisture within the meat, and this may lead to spoilage in storage. Taking this into account I do like to hot smoke brined-cured whole chicken. The skin hardens quickly and when cooked the meat remains moist. This makes for excellent eating either hot or cold.

If you choose to smoke only to enhance flavour, then both cold and hot methods will work; however curing meats prior to smoking will further improve their flavours. It is also better to air-dry meat for a few days before smoking it because this allows the meat to dry on the outer surface and allowing the smoke to stick to the meat more easily than to wet or moist surfaces.

If you choose smoking for preservation, i.e. to extend shelf life, then I recommend cold smoking.

Curing for a short time works well if you are only looking for flavour and produce with a short shelf life, but if you are hoping to preserve meat, then it is imperative you cure it for the appropriate time before smoking. Hot smoking at a high temperature results in the finished hot smoked meat being cooked by the end of the smoking process. A cold smoked product is considered to be uncooked.

The best tip I can give you is to think about the depth of flavour you require. If you prefer a deep smoked flavour, then consider smoking some sea salt and use this to dry-cure your meats as this will allow the smoky flavour to penetrate the meat during curing. You can also make a brine, or a concentrated wash with smoked sea salt and when used as a smoked wash this will add a timeless flavour to such products as fish roe, poached eggs, or even mozzarella cheese.

If you cure some lemons in a jar for a couple of months, you can use this as lemon salt (it's similar to making vanilla sugar except you are using lemons and salt). Now you can use it on its own to cure salmon giving it a nice citrus finish or you can smoke this too before curing meats like lamb, fish and vegetables, giving them a unique flavour. I bet that's got you and the Michelin star chefs thinking!

Whatever tools, equipment or storage facilities you use for smoking foods, you really need to dedicate them to smoking exclusively, because they can easily taint non-smoked food.

You can hot smoke on the top of your stove quite easily using such containers as an old pan, a Chinese wok, or even some ex-military mess tins. Just put a dessertspoonful of sawdust in the receptacle and a metal rack above the sawdust; place a fillet of fish on the rack and cover the pan with a lid or seal it with aluminium foil. Cook on low to medium heat for approximately 20mins and Hey Presto… luscious hot smoked fish! Don't worry about this indoor method filling your room with smoke, it does not happen if you do it correctly, but please act responsibly; have suitable extinguisher equipment to hand and make sure all available windows are open.

below: slicing a fillet of smoked salmon.

BARBECUE SMOKEHOUSE

With a £10 budget, you can move outdoors and use your existing barbecue, assuming it has a lid.

- Buy yourself a tin of baked beans and a small soldering iron from your local hardware store.

- Open your tin with a conventional opener being careful not to open more than ¾ of the way round the tin. The remaining ¼ will be used as a hinge.

- Having emptied, washed clean and dried the tin, make a hole in the hinge just big enough to take the soldering iron.

- Fill the tin with sawdust and close up the opening by carefully pushing the lid inward.

- Push the soldering iron through the small hole in the hinged lid and place tin and the soldering iron on the bottom rack of your barbecue.

- Arrange some meat on the rack above the tin, close the barbecue lid, and switch on your soldering iron. Smoke will come through the hole in the top and your meat will be ready within 45mins. However, the longer you leave it in the smoke the stronger it will taste.

How about having your own smokehouse?

Well, that can easily be achieved for under £200. Buy a budget-priced wooden shed from your local DIY store and erect it well away from anywhere that might be tainted by the smoke it generates. Attach dowelling rods inside across the width of the shed, or make a wooden framework to support some weld mesh that can sit easily on top of the frame, and from which you can hang your meat. Fit a metal sheet on the floor to help make it fireproof and on which you can stand one of those fancy garden chimneys, one that will hold sawdust to fuel and generate smoke. A few holes drilled in the top of the shed's back wall plus a few more in the bottom of its door will help with ventilation – and your smokehouse is ready for use.

Various fuels can be used for smoking. I prefer to use sawdust because when lit in a closed container, it only smoulders due to the oxygen supply being suppressed. This results in a continuous slow burn with plenty of time to complete its cycle. Wood chippings are prone to igniting and a fire can break out as a result of the oxygen in and around the fuel. Such fires also mean that the fuel burns out too quickly. Using sawdust especially when laid out in a trail similar to a maze will give you a continuous supply of released smoke for plenty of time to treat your meat.

You can add flavours to your smoke by placing herbs, spent barley malt, tea leaves or even seaweed on top of your sawdust. When added damp these flavourings help the sawdust to burn more slowly. Peat is one of my favourite sources of fuel; it offers a unique sweetness to the meat. Dung (that's right, cow pats and pats from such other livestock as sheep) can provide a sustainable slow-burning fuel that is often overlooked for smoking foodstuffs. It is, however, not for the faint-hearted.

Each smoker or smokehouse will have its own peculiarities. This, along with the fuel you use and how you use the smoker, combined with your tastes for flavour will all have a bearing on how long you smoke something. You can only determine the best timings by experimenting for yourself.

COLD SMOKING

To be classed as cold smoking the fire or heat source needs to be far enough away from the meat and, for the time it takes to reach the meat, for the smoke to have cooled down to the optimum temperatures of between 12°C and 30°C. Cold smoking should never be attempted if the external temperature exceeds 32°C. Preferably smoke in autumn and/or winter, unless you can replicate their conditions. You should aim for humidity levels of 80% or less. Placing a bowl of water in the smoker will help you to achieve this. I prefer cold smoking and I only eat hot smoked items within 3 days of their being smoked.

Some of my own timings and suggestions:

- Hot smoke a whole chicken until cooked (approx 2hrs) and one that has been brined overnight.

- Cold smoke sides of 24hr cured salmon for 1 whole day.

- Cold smoke 3-month-old salami sausage for at least 3 days, and whole 4-week-cured hams for at least 2 weeks using a brick-built smoker.

This final smoking method and timing suits my palate very well, because if my fire source ever goes out, I do not worry but just continue after re-lighting the fuel and ensuring there is enough for each day's burning. The only exception is to ensure the salmon gets at least 8hrs continuously in the smoke.

TOP TIP

I recommend the Bradley Smoker® for the hobbyist for both cold and hot smoking meat. This smoker fits most people's budget and is probably the best of its kind in the market place. But don't just take my word for it, check one out at **www.bradleysmoker.co.uk**

Let's draw a smoke screen …

Back in the early 1990s (which sounds strange now knowing it was in the last century), I was approached by a friend, the actress Daphne Neville (of *Bee the Otter* fame) who asked me to help raise awareness for a wildlife sanctuary based in Hillswick on the Shetland Isles in Scotland. The sanctuary did some excellent work in saving the Islands' wildlife, in particular the seal population, affected by the Braer Oil Disaster.

I did a lot of voluntary fund-raising that involved contacting companies who made specialist equipment to ask for such things as plumbing tools, stethoscopes and syringes, and organising rubber duck races to raise funds to send to Hillswick. One of these rubber duck races was held in Tewkesbury, Gloucestershire and whilst there I researched the Tewkesbury Ham, which was once cured and smoked in the Hop Pole Hotel. This got me really excited as the ham was smoked using peat and it is reputed to be the best of all smoked hams. Of course in years gone by, acquiring such a ham was more common, but trying to get a peat-smoked ham today is nigh on impossible, so another plan of action was required.

Well, I knew they still cut peat on the Shetlands so I asked the wildlife sanctuary if they still used it as a fuel source (not that I divulged why I was asking). When their answer was "yes", I made my mind up right there and then that I was going to deliver the goods and money I had raised for them personally, so I could get a chance to peat-smoke some ham in one of the chimneys on the Shetland Isles. Many weeks later I found myself hitching a free ride to the Isles on a charter plane courtesy of the Brent Oil Company. Once there I got on a bus at Lerwick and travelled north to Hillswick, where I was met by two of the sanctuary's volunteers who helped me with my

baggage and scurried me through the village to get me indoors and away from the appalling weather.

Inside the sanctuary I met the remaining staff and volunteers and handed over the raised monies and equipment to help them with their good work. They were enormously grateful and happy to receive it. I was pleased to see that most of the rooms in this large building, which was once the oldest pub on the Isles, had an open fire and were all burning peat. The smell hit me first, as burning peat has a distinctive and unique sweet aroma all of its own. I could not wait to ask if and when I could use one of the chimneys to smoke some ham. I really wanted to crack on! My stay was scheduled for 10 days and I had already spotted some extremely bendy drainage rods that would be ideal for helping me get my ham up a selected chimney. I could not explain how excited I was about peat smoking a ham but decided I would ask the house owner for her permission over dinner that evening. While the table was being set by the owner's two lovely daughters, one by one the remaining volunteers and staff started to appear, a total of 12 people including me. My first meal was about to be served when Jan the proprietor said: "We are all vegetarian here, I hope that won't be a problem for you!". She was of course referring to all the meals that would be served during my stay. She further explained that she was one of two people in the group who were vegan. My heart sank! I was mortified at what I had just heard. Of course, I never raised my question, not even my interest in charcuterie whilst I was there. I took the news as a reminder that I was there to help out with their cause, not mine, so I bit the bullet and gave them my all for the remaining time I spent there.

During my stay Jan asked the group if anyone felt they could skin a dead otter that was lying in her freezer so that the pelt could be cured and used for educational purposes. The otter had been run over by an army Land Rover on Unst, the northern-most part of the Isles, and although the soldiers had raced for many hours to bring the injured otter to the wildlife sanctuary, it had died en route. Without explaining my skill, I volunteered to give it a go and without further ado the otter was taken out of the freezer and left to defrost. Of all the animals that I have skinned, this was certainly the toughest; negotiating my knife around webbed feet and a long thick tail was the most difficult part, but the job was done. Jan remarked on my skills and asked "Are you sure you haven't done this before?". As it was my first otter, I could honestly answer "No, never". I did not have the heart to disclose to the vegan owner of this wildlife sanctuary that she had a highly skilled butcher with an interest in blood sports staying under her roof!

On leaving Hillswick, I couldn't wait to get to the airport at Lerwick to get a protein fix, for I was suffering from flatulence as a result of the vegetarian diet I had been on since the start of my stay. I reached the airport cafeteria and asked the lady behind the counter for "Two bacon butties and a coffee", she replied in broad Scots "Sorree me luv, we hav nay bayconn, the plane from Eberdeeeen wi oor supplies has nay arrived yet, due tu thee bad weather thee nose, aye it's a shame". With my mouth wide open in disbelief at what I was hearing, I just stood there in a moment's silence – only to be broken when I suddenly farted, very, very loudly!

PORK

Well, we've covered the blood, offal and ham, so now let's talk pork because without pigs the world would be so different. Can you imagine the full English breakfast without black pudding, sausage and bacon, or your mid-week or Sunday roast pork joint without the crackling? Each breed of pig offers a taste different from that of the other breeds, as will become clear when you make your way through the traditional breeds on your culinary tour of *charcuterie.*

As breakfast has already been mentioned, this would be a good place to introduce the sausage, a product governed by thousands of recipes from around the world and one that comes in many forms: short, long, thin, thick, round, square or skinless; and in several colours too. There are many books on the market that specifically cover sausage making in its entirety, so I'll just deal with a few points here to whet your taste buds.

One important point I must get across early in this chapter is one I have mentioned before in the chapter on fat: you need to work from a good base when making sausage.

I strongly suggest that you start with a ratio of 60% meat: 40% fat, but never less than a 70:30 ratio. An easy way to visualise and understand this method is to always assume that any shoulder pork contains 30% fat, of which 18% is hidden and 12% is visible. Belly pork has around 40% fat, so when you put equal amounts of pork together from both of these areas then you are close enough to having your 60:40 ratio. Of course this is only a guide and not an accurate measure but, trust me, it is the best way to start your sausage making career. From here you can always add or take away fat to suit your preference.

above: Oxford, Sandy & Black.

I know I have mentioned this more than once, but I am convinced that the best pig for both pork and sausages is the Gloucester Old Spot. This breed offers sweet-tasting meat, soft in texture with enough fat to provide a flavour superior to that of any other breed. This breed is sometimes known as the 'orchard pig', as the black spots on its back are supposed to resemble bruises from falling apples in the orchards of the beautiful county of Gloucestershire. These pigs are not just docile, they are also territorial, for if they break out of their enclosure you are sure to find them just feet away from their pen, either rooting for food or fast asleep! They have coarse waxy hair that is waterproof; this means they can continue rooting for food in the rain, unlike other breeds that will run for cover quite quickly.

Bringing home the bacon!

In France I had a Gloucester Old Spot sow called Belle, whom I took for daily walks down the many lanes leading from our farm. Here she could eat beech mast and acorns in the tree-lined lanes that offered shade as well as food. I found these strolls were very therapeutic and amusing because I could tap Belle on her left shoulder and she would turn to the right, or tap her on her right shoulder for her to turn to the left. This entertained my French neighbours who, even though they were country folk, had never seen such a spectacle.

I also kept Tamworths – ginger pigs that certainly kept you on your toes – they were bright, inquisitive and sometimes downright naughty. When those pigs got out from their enclosure you knew you were in for at least a marathon, or even a 'Krypton Factor' style assault course, just to get them back into their pen. They took great joy in exploring the county at high speed. I recall that during a spell of very hot weather we were unable to keep their water buckets filled up, as they would overturn them immediately in order to wallow in the mud they created. There was a natural spring in the next field, so I thought it wise to erect a pen that included the spring within the enclosure. I had just finished making this with my 9-year-old son when I asked him to go back to the farm, herd up the Tamworths and bring them down to the new pen while I took a short rest. He was gone for some time, but I thought nothing of it, assuming he had gone to get himself a drink, as it was a very hot day. In fact the delay was due to the Tamworths having run amok as soon as their gate was opened to release them! Unbeknown to me they had run off in different directions and my wife was running down the lanes rounding them up. Well, at this point I was dozing under a tree, whose overhanging canopy was shielding me from the burning sun, when all of a sudden I heard my wife hollering "C'mon piggies, C'mon little piggies," and, like a mirage, I could see through the mid-day heat haze, my wife marching towards me followed by our herd of Tamworths. She was wearing green wellies and had a shepherd's crook in one hand and a bucket of feed in the other. Then I had to rub my eyes because she was wearing nothing but her bra and knickers!!!! What a sight! My wife, by the way, is well endowed and to see her herding these near wild pigs was a real picture. My French neighbours once again thought we were absolutely bonkers, but I have to say that whenever I hear the expression: 'Bringing home the bacon' I recall the vision of my wife herding those Tamworths into their new pen. (It would be useful to have a photograph or an illustration for this story, however if you don't mind, I'll keep this one to myself.)

(Sorry darling, the publisher must have slipped this one in without my knowledge … but, but … darling, I do love you!)

SAUSAGE MAKING

I'm assuming some of you who are reading this book already know how to make sausage, so I will just offer a basic method here for those of you who have not yet travelled into this magnificent culinary field. I could easily write a book on sausage making and recipes.

To get you started on the road to discovery I suggest you have the following equipment and ingredients ready:

- Grinder or food processor
- Large mixing bowl
- Sausage filler
- Glass measuring jug
- Kitchen knife

Ingredients

2kg pork shoulder
2.5m boar casings (also known as sausage skins)
1 packet of sage and onion stuffing (seasoning)
100ml water

Method

1. Having assembled your equipment and ingredients, place your casings in water to soak, because after being packed in salt they will need to re-hydrate.
2. Cut the meat into pieces small enough to pass through the grinder. If you do not have a grinder ask your local butcher for minced shoulder of pork for sausage making. Pass the meat through the grinder into the mixing bowl.
3. Start adding seasoning and water constantly mixing until the mixture is well combined and tacky to the touch.
4. Make a small patty and cook it to test that batch of meat.
5. If you are satisfied that the seasoning in the cooked patty is OK, load the sausage filler with the mix.
6. Place (shire) the casings onto the filler spout, and fill the skins **loosely**. At all costs avoid over-stuffing the casings or they will be prone to split and you will be unable to link them.

Congratulations! You have just made your first sausages!! All that is left now is for you to either link them or just cut off a length, as you need it. The following recipes show you just a few of the variations available.

'Lorne' or 'Square' Sausage

One of the easiest sausages to make, these are often found at breakfast time in Scotland, but are less known south of Hadrian's Wall.

Ingredients (to make 1.5–2kg sausage)

500g beef (minced)
500g pork (minced)
225g fine oats
1 tsp salt
1 tsp white pepper
1 tsp coriander
½ nutmeg (freshly grated)
¼ tsp mace
250ml water

I would hazard a guess that once upon a time in bonny Scotland there was a shortage of casings so the canny Scots decided to put their sausage mix into a terrine or loaf tin. Once chilled, the set meat could be sliced and cooked as a skinless square sausage. Of course, any sausage recipe can be made in this way, but if you wish to use the traditional method you should consider a 50:50 pork and beef mix using mace, nutmeg, salt and pepper as your main seasoning ingredients at the rate of 25g per kilo of meat. Once mixed, you could, if you wish, place sheets of greaseproof paper between the slices and freeze them until required.

There are two more British skinless sausages that I know, one is the **Oxford sausage**, which comprises: 33% pork shoulder, 33% veal and 33% belly pork, with mace, nutmeg, salt and pepper as seasoning. You can, of course, add 5% breadcrumbs or rusk, or more if you prefer, to the mix along with some mixed herbs to add flavour and to bulk up the sausage. I can see why the traditional Oxford sausages taste so nice, if the pork comes from an Oxford Sandy Black pig, it will taste as good as a Gloucester Old Spot which, in my opinion, is the best of all the traditional breeds. I know that statement will provoke debate and disappoint some people, but to me it's like saying the Oxford Sandy Black resembles a Hungarian *Mangalitza*.

Plain Pork Sausage

The best 'all time, anytime' sausage. The meat should be 50% pork shoulder and 50% pork belly. Overall 70% meat and 30% fat is a good guide.

1kg of finished mix should produce 12–14 sausages
Preparation time 30mins

Ingredients

Use the following combined seasoning mix at a ratio of 25g per kilo of meat:
100g salt
50g sage
100g pepper
10g mace
200g sugar – honey works well with this one (optional)
Pinch saltpetre (optional)
200g rusk (see explanation below) or breadcrumbs
475ml water

Even though there is a lot of pepper in the mix I still gave myself a score of 7 out of 10 for this recipe. Alternatively use a seasoning mix of 85% salt, 10% white pepper along with 5% nutmeg and starting with 20g per kilo of meat adjust to your liking (I scored this version 8 out of 10). You need to evolve your own recipe by adding or subtracting ingredients.

TOP TIP

1   For all sausage mixes, before filling the casings, make a patty of the mix and lightly fry to sample for taste – then adjust the seasoning accordingly.

2   Sausages will taste better if allowed to age overnight so that the seasoning can permeate the meat thoroughly.

3   Rusk is hard breadcrumbs that have been baked to kill the yeast. If you are using fresh breadcrumbs, then consider baking them first to avoid the yeast reacting with the meat through fermentation.

Method

1   Mince the meat once, add all the other ingredients, mix well.

2   Mince again.

3   If preferred you can further bind the mix in a mixing bowl using a dough hook.

4   Fill the mix into 28mm natural boar casings.

5   Pack the sausages in sixes on a black sausage tray ready to be over-wrapped with cling film.

Glamorgan Sausage (*Selsig Morgannwg*)

This skinless Welsh sausage is actually meatless. I include it here purely and simply because it tastes divine. It consists predominately of leeks, cheese and breadcrumbs, and is a skinless sausage suitable for vegetarians. This truly great recipe originates from Glamorgan in Wales.

Serves 4–6
Preparation time 30mins

Ingredients

200g Caerphilly cheese

200g golden breadcrumbs or 150g rusk and 50g golden breadcrumbs for coating

1 leek

2 eggs

1 tsp English mustard powder

Parsley and sage (chopped)

Salt and pepper to taste

Method

1 Mix all the ingredients together, leaving 50g of the breadcrumbs in which to roll the sausages before cooking.

2 After mixing and shaping into sausage shapes, roll the mix through flour and a little beaten egg.

3 Roll in the remaining breadcrumbs.

4 Gently fry in butter until cooked.

Digressing I know, but when asking for sausage skins in France, think of Wales! Because in French, sausage skins are called *boyaux* pronounced '*boyo*' as in the Welsh vernacular 'is nit?'.

Caution! Joke coming …

"Can I have some Irish sausages, please?" asked the Irishman, walking up to the counter.

The assistant looked at him and asked: "Are you Irish?"

"If I had asked you for Italian sausage, would you ask me if I was Italian?" demanded the Irishman indignantly.

"Or if I asked for German Bratwurst, would you ask if I was German?"

Then warming to his theme, he went on: "Or if I asked you for a Kosher hot-dog, would you ask me if I am Jewish?"

"Oh if I asked you for a taco, would you ask me if I was Mexican? Would you? Would you?"

The assistant said, "Well, no Sir."

Suitably encouraged by the success of his logic, the Irishman steps it up a gear.

"And if I were to ask you for frogs legs, would you ask me if I was French?"

"What about Danish Bacon, would you ask me if I was Danish?"

"Well no, I definitely wouldn't" conceded the assistant.

So, now bursting with righteous indignation, the Irishman says: "Well alright then, why did you ask me if I'm Irish, was it because I asked for Irish sausages?"

The assistant replied, "No Sir, it's because you are here at **TOYS-R-US**."

Pork & Stilton
or *Porc et Roquefort*

These are two sausages that I make regularly, especially at Christmas time, when I add about 10–15% of either cheese to my plain pork sausage mix. Once made, I simmer the sausages for 15mins in water, lightly brown them in a skillet and then leave to cool. I wrap thick slices of dry-cured bacon around each chilled sausage and stand them upright in a Kilner® jar topped up with dripping. These I give away as Christmas presents to my friends who relish this available 'mini feast'. This was one product the French were pleasantly amazed to find – a fresh sausage with cheese added as a main ingredient. I seem to remember their expression was something like "Ooh la, la!".

'********** Sausage'

I have invented sausages many times but only occasionally are the recipes good enough for others to use willingly. One of those I would like to tell you about became known as the… . Well, let's see if you can guess the name as I give you the clues. It is a pork-based sausage, whose inspiration came from a Lowry painting of match stalk men and match stalk cats and dogs. Have you guessed the name yet? No? OK, then let's give you some more clues. In the pork mix are additional pieces of chopped black pudding. No, not a Lancashire sausage, but you are so close. If it were to be pork and black pudding then – yes it would be called a Lancashire sausage, however you are in the right county but there is one further ingredient. Think back to the Lowry painting. Yes! We need to add the chimney smoke and adding smoky bacon bits does this and the sausage then became known as the … ? I'll have to put you out of your misery, it is known as the Manchester Sausage. Some years later, in a recipe book, I found a Manchester Sausage whose ingredients differ from mine. Unfortunately this recipe was published before I had invented my sausage. Just shows you can't win them all, perhaps I should rename mine the Lowry Sausage!

Porc et Truffe

This sausage has a great combination of flavour and texture. It is a sausage that I often made in the village where I lived in France. The villagers occasionally found one of these precious fungi and would present it to me to add to sausages made from the *Cul Noir Limousin Cochon* that loosely translates as the 'black-arsed pig from the Limousin region' – which bordered on the village. The *Cul Noir* are similar to our Saddleback in markings, however they are slow-growing and can take up to 18 months to mature and be ready for the table. Adding black pudding or even chopped sweet prunes can also make sausages with black speckles. Just add enough to complement the pork, anything up to 10% of the total ingredients. However, if using strong pungent ingredients like truffles, then less than 5% will be sufficient.

Winston Churchill

A name I once gave a sausage dish that dates back to the time of World War II when, during the frequent food shortages, people were actively encouraged to find different ways to make food interesting. One such dish involved a potato cored like an apple and stuffed with a protruding sausage. The picture of this simple dish reminded me of Winston Churchill smoking one of his famous cigars.

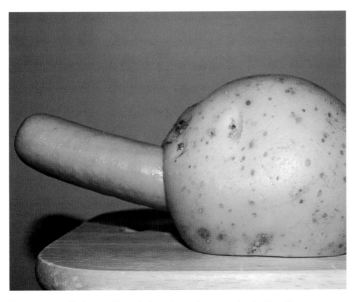

OK, my attempt looks more like a duck, but you get my meaning don't you?

NOTE

Did you know that 'bangers' got their name from sausages produced in wartime? They were made with too much water and tended to explode in the frying pan when the water reacted with the hot fat.

Whale meat was used readily during the war years as it was not on ration like other meats. So much of it was eaten in London that a young lady called Vera Lynn sang a song about it and it went something like this: "Whale meat again, don't know where, don't know when" … that's the good thing about this book – you never know when a laugh is coming.

Cumberland Sausage

Originally made from pork that came from the Cumberland pig, this sausage is traditionally made in the form of a ring or 'twirl'. The Cumberland pig is now extinct, so the sausage will never be the same again. However, good sausages are still made to the original recipe apart from the Cumberland pork. The recipe uses a seasoning mix of 75% salt and 25% black pepper, once again at a ratio of 25g per kilo of coarsely chopped meat. Use 34mm casings.

Lincolnshire Sausage

Like the Cumberland sausage, these will remain a favourite in my home, but sadly they too can no longer be made authentically. Like the Cumberland, the Lincolnshire pig is now extinct. The Lincolnshires were curly coated animals that looked like pigs in sheep's clothing (probably their downfall). To make Lincolnshire sausage, follow the plain pork recipe; add mace, sugar, basil and oregano, remembering to grind the pork to a fine texture before mixing in the seasoning and herbs. They are best in boar casings of 28mm or in lamb casings of 22mm+.

above: Cumberland sausage

Chipolatas

Easily made by following the plain pork sausage recipe minced finely. Instead of using boar casings use lamb skins to acquire instantly recognisable thin sausages. Even though the recipe mix is the same as for plain pork, finishing them in lamb casings makes for a different flavour.

Pork & Leek

A great sausage that is easily put together, using plain pork sausage seasoning with a little celery salt added. Allow four leeks to a basic 10kg mix.

Method

1 Wash and cut the leeks lengthways into quarters, then chop into small pieces and blanche by simmering in water until soft.

2 Drain the leeks but retain the water and allow both to cool.

3 Fold the cooked leeks into the sausage mix and add the cooled cooking water. If you try to add leeks without cooking them first, they will be too hard and have sharp edges that are likely to pierce the casings and burst the sausage.

4 As with all sausages, add rusk or breadcrumbs if you wish.

Pork, Leek & Potato

Made in exactly the same way as Pork & Leek, but with the addition of mashed potato and fried onion; this to me is bubble and squeak in a sausage. Both of these sausages are best in casings of between 30 and 34mm that show off the fillings proudly. I believe this one originated in Lincolnshire, but I have no evidence other than the lady who gave it to me in France explaining that it was often made by her local butcher back home in Lincolnshire. (I know what you are saying: "Bubble and Squeak is traditionally made with cabbage", but do remember to be inventive – sometimes breaking the rules means success!)

Chorizo ('choreetho')

A semi air-dried sausage that is, in my opinion, hugely under-estimated and not used enough in our everyday cooking repertoire. It can be used in many places. On pizza is probably a favourite, while sliced chunks in a *cassoulet* or a hot soup really work well, as they do in pasta dishes and rice dishes such as paella. Recently I have seen it sold hot in Borough Market in London, where one of the stallholders offers a toasted bread roll filled with a grilled *chorizo* split lengthways along with roasted red peppers and a dressed salad. The queue for this feast was more than 20 deep! Does that tell you something?

TOP TIP

Replacing some of the water in the mix with olive oil plus a few shakes of Tabasco® sauce works very well.

Chorizo

The basic *chorizo* recipe is the same as for plain pork, but replace the sage and mace with cayenne pepper, paprika and garlic. *Chorizo* can be put in 36mm boar casings.

Another, and probably my favourite, *chorizo* recipe is this semi air-dried sausage that, unlike salami, is not left to develop a white powdery mould on the surface.

Ingredients

7.5kg pork
1.5kg beef
240g salt
24g saltpetre
20g ground black pepper
10g nutmeg
10g hot chilli powder
40g paprika
280g mild chilli powder
100ml olive oil

Method

1 Trim the meat thoroughly, discarding any sinews.
2 Mince using a 5–6mm plate.
3 Add and blend the seasoning to the meat mix.
4 Fill 34–36mm boar casings and make to length, approximately 50cm.
5 Tie the two ends together using a fine butchers twine.
6 Pre air-dry at 25°C (77°F) for 6hrs, then air-dry for about 2 weeks at a constant 15°C (60°F) and 80% humidity.
7 The shelf life will be several weeks from the end of the drying stage.
8 Wiping with olive oil before sale or serving will enhance the appearance and colour of the sausages.

Bratwurst

A sausage I have made, sold and eaten too many times too mention, and often whilst I lived and worked in Germany. At the Bratwurst Museum in Holzhausen near Arnstadt in the old East Germany I have eaten the original *Thuringen Bratwurst*, which is unsurpassed, except perhaps by the smaller *Nurnburger Bratwurst*.

Small chorizo

A large *chorizo* can be made using 54mm ox casings and with added back fat cut into thumbnail-sized pieces, add just enough to offer an alternative texture to the main mix. Of course the pre-drying and drying times need to be extended for the larger version. Once mature this *chorizo* can be served as thin slices.

TOP TIP

When making air-dried or *salami* sausage it is best to remove all visible silver skin and sinews. Silver skin is the fine bluish film of skin you find in between the joint of two muscles; the outer skin on a tenderloin demonstrates this well. Use only trimmed lean meat, then add back the fat to the mix before seasoning. Experiment with any recipe that takes your fancy – you will be surprised and may be delighted with your efforts.

Ingredients

(1) 2kg pork
4 eggs
Rusk to taste
Milk to taste
40g salt
5g white pepper
1 pinch cumin
1 pinch nutmeg

(2) 4kg veal
4kg pork
6–10 eggs
1ltr milk
200g salt
30g white pepper
10g cumin
10g nutmeg

(3) The *bratwurst* I enjoy the most is seasoned with the following ingredients for every kilo of meat used:

18g salt
2g white pepper
2g marjoram
2g lemon zest
1g mace
1g ginger

Recipe for stags

I'm often asked to demonstrate sausage-making and to share some of its secrets with students. I enjoy this as much as eating sausage itself – seeing the joy on the unsuspecting faces of the students as they discover the art of creating such splendour is vastly rewarding. On one such occasion I was asked to teach a group of 22 young men who were together for a Stag Party to celebrate the bridegroom's remaining freedom before his wedding. The group had travelled to Somerset from London by train and were all dressed in pink, each wearing a set of plastic pig ears and a snout to match. They were a sight for sore eyes I can tell you! The groom was dressed as a *Bratwurst im Brotchen* – a hot dog to you and me.

I was to teach them sausage-making for several hours before they ate their wares on a barbecue, prior to returning to London by train to embrace the city nightlife and their awaiting casks of beer. The men were split into several groups and were handed envelopes containing the first sausage recipe they had to follow to win prizes for the best sausage maker and sausage linker. The groom and his group received a sealed envelope containing the following recipe. The translation, via their Blackberry phones, created great mirth amongst the group. So – go on, have some fun, try translating the recipe for yourself and I hope you enjoy it as much as the bridegroom and his friends did on that strange and wonderful day.

Deutsche Bratwurst

Rezept

Zwei und halb kilo Schweine fleisch
Viermal Eier
Zwieback zum abschmecken
Milch zum abschmecken
Vierzig gramm Saltz
Fünf gramm weiser Pfeffer
Eine prise Kreuzkummel
Eine prise Muskat

Methode

1 Legen sie das fleisch zweimal durch eine wolfe/muhle, hinzufugen die eier, gewurz und die zwieback und milch zu kosten. Jetzt mischung zusammen und fullen schwein feller von vier und dreizig millimetre.

2 Zu kochen: Ersten langsam kochen die wurst in wasser für fünfzehen minuten dann abschliessend grillen bis braun.

Boudin Blanc

One of the finest white sausages in the world and again we have to thank the French. Below is the recipe for a classic 6kg *boudin blanc* mix.

Makes 24–26 sausages
Preparation time 60mins

Ingredients

3.5ltr milk (infused with a
  bouquet garni for 2hrs)
6kg fatty pork
6 whole eggs
24 egg whites
100g flour
200g salt
25g white pepper
36mm boar casings

Method

1 Mince the pork or use a bowl chopper if you have access to one.
2 Add and mix all the other ingredients together.
3 Fill boar casings (36mm minimum).
4 Cook in a large pot of water at a steady 85°C for 30mins keeping the sausage submerged.
5 Serve hot or cold.

The best thing about *boudin blanc* is you can make some very exciting variations. Here are a few ideas for you to think about:

Rabbit and Leek

Rabbit and Rocket

Foie Gras and Truffles

Smoked Salmon and Quail Eggs (boiled and chopped)

Shellfish

Veal and Ham

Prune and Pistachio

Vodka and Apricot

I do hope you allow yourself to be creative and are able to serve some of these variations at one of your next barbecues.

As I mentioned earlier, I could write a book about sausages, but I think I should stop here and move on to some more exciting pork products.

Rillons

This is a dish we British do not embrace for some reason, yet the French laud it as we do a good pork pie.

2–3 pieces per person
Preparation time 15mins
Cooking time 2–3hrs

Ingredients

2kg belly pork
2kg lard or dripping
Salt and pepper to taste
Paprika (optional)

TOP TIP

Rillons can also be stored like *Confit de Porc* in Kilner® jars covered in dripping. They will keep for several months in a larder without refrigeration and are ideal as picnic food.

Method

1 Cut several 5–6cm square pieces from a slice of belly pork.
2 Season with salt, pepper and a little paprika.
3 Brown in a skillet.
4 Once browned, place in a stew pot and cover the meat with at least 1in of dripping, then cook slowly for 2–3hrs or until tender.
5 Once cooked, either eat warm, or leave to cool and eat with a salad.

Pork & Pistachio Pâté

A pâté I have made several times and one I found very useful when I had unsold sausages leftover in my shop.

This terrine looks great when sliced and the green pistachio nuts glisten while adding flavour, texture and character.

Preparation time 30mins
Cooking time 60mins

Ingredients

Leftover sausages
3–4 pistachio nuts per sausage used
12 slices of streaky bacon

Method

1 Grease a terrine and line it with streaky bacon.
2 Remove the skins from the sausages.
3 Add pistachio nuts to the forcemeat and mix well.
4 Fill the terrine with the mixture, then fold over the bacon and cook in a *bain-marie*.

Crépinette

Serves 6 (ideally 2 per person)
Preparation time 30mins
Cooking time 6–8mins

Ingredients

1kg pork mince
Season to taste with salt, pepper and mixed
   dried herbs
Alternatively use any leftover forcemeat

Method

1 Finely mince the pork with the herbs.
2 Form into 100g patties similar in shape
   to soft, round-cornered, triangular Hash
   Browns.
3 Place a pitted prune, dried apricot, sage
   leaf or chopped fresh parsley on each
   patty and wrap in caul fat.
4 Gently sauté until cooked.
5 Serve with fresh bread and a side dish
   of *dauphinoise* potatoes and baby
   vegetables.

Rillette de Porc

Preparation time 30mins
Cooking time 6–8hrs

Ingredients

2kg pork
2kg lard or dripping
Salt and pepper to taste
Nutmeg (optional)

Method

1 Dice lean pork into approximately 5cm
   cubes.
2 As for *rillons* (see above) place in a stew
   pot or an electric slow cooker and cover
   in dripping by at least 5cm.
3 Cook slowly for about 6–8hrs or longer
   if required.
4 When the meat is tender to the point of
   falling apart, turn off the heat.
5 Take out the cubed pork and shred with
   two forks, this is time-consuming but well
   worth the effort. (You could, if you wish,
   pound the meat in a large heavy pestle and
   mortar, or as a last resort, use a blender –
   but only pulse briefly.)
6 Season the shredded meat with salt,
   pepper and a little nutmeg.
7 Add the cooking juices and dripping until
   you are happy with the consistency.
8 Pot into ramekins, or a larger dish of your
   choice.

TOP TIP

When potting your meat, aim for a wet
bog consistency, i.e. when pressed, the
juices rise to the surface immediately.
However, if you intend to store your potted
meat, cover with at least 4–5cm of lard.

Toad in the Hole

A great budget meal.

Serves 4–6
Preparation time 5mins
Cooking time 30mins

Ingredients

12 sausages
6 eggs and equal volumes of milk and plain flour
1 pinch salt

Method

1 Part-cook your chosen sausage in a deep baking tray with some dripping.

2 Mix together the eggs, milk, flour and salt.

3 When the dripping becomes really hot, add your Yorkshire Pudding batter mix.

4 Cook for a further 25mins or until the batter has risen and is a golden brown colour.

5 Serve with your favourite gravy.

FLASHBACK 16

Saucy sausages

I have for many years travelled most of Europe where I have taught my craft to those who have been willing to pay, or have offered something in return, such as an overnight stay in their hotel, or a free dinner for two. Sometimes I have taught for nothing at all, as when I have taken a shine to the person and perhaps seen something in them that pleased me – even something as simple as good manners and respect for others. Well, on one such occasion I found myself at the Hopton Arms in Herefordshire teaching the new chef, Marina. This lady from Wales had entered the culinary world late in life, she was full of passion for her trade and wanted to gain some *charcuterie* experience to broaden her range of skills. I agreed to go along and meet Marina and, as she impressed me with her willingness to learn, it was decided I would give her several one-on-one lessons on certain aspects of *charcuterie* starting with sausage-making.

Sausage-making is a great icebreaker and demonstrates how patient, capable and dextrous your pupil can be. Marina was all of these and she had a fantastic sense of humour that enabled us both to quickly get on with each other in a very relaxed way. I have to tell you here that, given the opportunity, I am a dreadful flirt; harmless I must admit, for I would do nothing to spoil what I have with my wife, but nevertheless a dreadful flirt, I am.

As you can imagine, sausage-making lessons with a lady chef is bound to be flirtatious and right from the off there was laughter. As I proceeded to teach Marina this art form she would frequently remark, "Oh! Bryn would like this" and occasionally "Oh! Bryn would like that", (Bryn, by the way, is Marina's partner, also from Wales and whom I was yet to meet). I must say I was a little intrigued about Bryn; would Bryn be a huge ex-rugby player from the valleys, or as vast as Bryn Terfel, the Welsh opera singer who sings with such giants as Andrea Bocelli? Either way I thought I should be careful about my flirtatious manner. Holding back lasted about 5 minutes and I continued to tease Marina throughout our lesson, including remarking on how small her hands are, saying "Look at your small hands, they will make any man feel proud" whilst she was getting to grips with linking the sausage. Of course I was being very suggestive, and she just laughed and laughed at all my innuendoes, which encouraged me all the more.

Eventually the *charcuterie* lesson came to an end for that day and, as we proceeded to clean up after ourselves, Marina suddenly announced that Bryn was in the bar and that she would like to introduce me. The kitchen was clean and with the sausage we had just made hanging in the walk-in fridge to mature, we were finished and ready for some refreshment. We proceeded for a well-deserved pint of real ale in this popular and obviously very busy bar, here several staff were working and many customers were enjoying their favourite tipples. A very attractive, slender brunette with a cheery smile was pulling my pint. I couldn't keep my eyes off her. She then walked towards me with my pint and said in a nice soft Welsh accent, "Hi, nice to meet you Marc-Frederic, I hear you have earned this pint. Oh! By the way I'm Bren, but you can call me Brenda if you wish." I had absolutely no idea! Serves me right, what a donkey I am!

Sausage Croissants

Great fun to make and experiment with.

Serves 6
Preparation time 30mins
Cooking time 20–30mins

Ingredients

400g puff pastry
6 small sausages
Egg wash

Method

1 Brown 6 small sausages (*Nuremburgers* are ideal) in a skillet.
2 Roll the pastry (I use a ready-made puff pastry) into a 10in diameter circle.
3 Divide into six triangular pieces.
4 Place a small browned sausage at the broad end of the pastry and roll until the point meets up with the rest.
5 Brush with an egg wash.
6 Bake in a preheated oven at 180°C for 20mins or until golden brown.

Another version includes baked triangular pieces of red pepper placed onto the pastry along with a cooked Merguez sausage, and then rolled and sealed. Cook as above.

Sausage Rolls

One of my favourite and easily made picnic / party foods.

Preparation time 45mins
Cooking time 30mins

Q: How do you make a sausage roll?

A: Push it down a slope!

Ingredients

500g puff pastry
1kg pork (finely minced)
1 onion (finely chopped or blended)
1 tbsp brown sugar
Salt and pepper to taste
Mixed herbs (optional)
Egg wash

TOP TIP

For an extra bite add small chopped pieces of chorizo to the forcemeat mixture. Or go mad and make different mixtures such as pork and apricot, pork and apple or pork with chopped walnuts and Stilton.

Method

1   First make the forcemeat; for each kilo of finely minced pork add 1 onion finely chopped or pulped in a blender along with 1 tbsp light brown sugar, finely chopped sage and salt and white pepper to taste.

2   Make your own puff pastry (see page 180), or buy it ready-made.

3   Roll out the pastry and divide into equal strips each being 12cm wide.

4   Place pork forcemeat mixture onto the pastry like a long sausage lying on a blanket waiting to be wrapped up and tucked into bed.

5   Brush the pastry edges with a milk or egg wash, fold over the pastry and crimp together.

6   Brush the pastry roll with the remaining wash.

7   Divide into equal lengths before scoring the tops with a knife.

8   Bake in an oven preheated to 160°C for 25mins or until the pastry turns golden brown.

Leftover Parcels

They deserve a better name, maybe Magic Parcels or even *Surprise en Croûte*? You see, after each batch of sausage rolls there always seems to be a little pastry left over. I use whatever is lying around in my fridge to make parcel fillings – the ingredients could be anything. Only recently after a sausage roll session I found some raw onion, sausage mix, sliced tomato and Philadelphia® soft cheese. I put them all in a 'parcel', brought the corners together and crimped the joints so it looked like a cardinal's biretta hat and then baked it alongside my sausage rolls. The result was absolutely scrumptious! Some of these parcels are fought over amongst family members, so it might pay to bake a few extra!

Scotch Eggs

Invented at Fortnum and Mason's store in London back in 1738, they have been popular ever since their creation. Back then coach travellers required snacks to help suppress their hunger as they travelled to and from the city. Andrea Tanner, the company Archivist, explained that pullet (that's a teenage chicken to you and me) eggs were predominately used then, with pork forcemeat seasoned with nutmeg, pepper and chopped parsley. The name was taken from the pullet eggs being 'scotched' meaning bastardised, i.e. changed in form.

A past client of mine whom I used to visit often, would feed me these savouries if I happened to manage my visit near lunchtime. (Strange that, I never visited Penny before 11:30am on any day that I delivered there, always unintentionally of course!) She has an extraordinary talent for making Scotch Eggs, so good that she, and her husband Neil Chambers, formed The Handmade Scotch Egg Company® in Herefordshire. The one piece of advice I remember being given by Penny was to deep-fat fry the eggs in groundnut oil because it has different heating properties from other oils and this enables the forcemeat to cook right through whilst the bread crumbed casing remains intact and golden in colour. **www.handmadescotcheggs.co.uk**

Serves 6
Preparation time 30mins
Cooking time 6–8mins

Ingredients

6 eggs
800g forcemeat
Egg wash
Breadcrumbs

TOP TIP

Cooking times may vary according to the size of eggs used.

Method

1 Place the eggs in a pan of cold water; bring to the boil for an overall cooking time of no more than 10mins.

2 Once hard-boiled, rinse and peel the eggs under cold water and leave to dry on a paper kitchen towel.

3 Roll the dry eggs in seasoned flour and wrap them in 120g of seasoned forcemeat.

4 Roll the eggs in seasoned flour again, then in a saucer of beaten egg wash.

5 Finally roll in another saucer of breadcrumbs.

6 Deep fry in nut oil for 6–8mins at 180°C or until golden brown.

Hand-Raised Game Pie

Another in-house product that Fortnum and Mason supplied to the many coach travellers that frequently passed their premises on journeys to and from the big city. These pies would be sliced and returned to the tins in which they were cooked and then covered in muslin to keep away any flies and the dust created by the large coach wheels on the busy roads out of London.

Preparation time 45mins
Cooking time 90mins

Ingredients

To fill an 8in pie mould
500g forcemeat
(traditionally a
combination or selection
of hare, pigeon, duck,
goose and rabbit but
always with some pork,
as that provided the fat
required to keep the
pie moist)
1kg mixed game meat
Hot water pastry
Salt and pepper to taste
Mixed herbs finely chopped
(optional)

Method

1 Make your hot water pastry (recipe page 181) and leave for 4hrs or overnight to cool but avoid putting it into a fridge, as the pastry should be supple and pliable enough to work. (Just because it is made with hot water and is called a hot water pastry this does not mean you have to work with it whilst it is still hot.)

2 Prepare the forcemeat by adding seasoning of your choice and leave to stand overnight to allow the flavours to permeate.

3 Next morning allow the pastry to come to room temperature.

4 In the meantime choose a pie mould, grease with lard, and dust with plain flour.

5 Sort the game ingredients in descending order, with what is likely to be the driest of meats first.

6 Throw ¾ of the pastry into the pie mould, press down into the edges and then start hand raising the pastry to the upper edges of the mould. (Yes, that is why it is called hand-raised pastry!)

7 Into the completed pastry case put a layer of the driest game meat, e.g. venison.

8 Add a layer of forcemeat, followed by a layer of pheasant, another layer of forcemeat, and finally some pigeon and a topping of more forcemeat. Layering the meat in this way will allow the fat in the forcemeat to cook out and baste the drier meats within the mould. Make a lid from the remaining ¼ mix of pastry and dress with a few decorated pastry leaves.

9 Place in an oven preheated to 180°C for 20mins.

10 Turn the heat down to 160°C for a further 60mins.

11 Take the pie out of the oven and allow it to cool for a while (up to 40mins if you are using an oval fluted pie mould) as this will prevent the pie collapsing.

12 Take off the mould, egg wash the pie and return it to a hot oven for a further 20mins to brown.

13 Once the cooked pie is chilled add gelatine through the top of the piecrust and allow it to set before serving.

Pork Pie (*Pâté en Croûte*)

This is sometimes called a Stand Pie, especially in Yorkshire. However, regardless of the name, this is certainly one of Britain's culinary classics. Definitely helped by Melton Mowbray putting this great pie on our food map.

Preparation time 60mins
Cooking time 90mins

Ingredients

Hot water pastry (follow recipe on page 181)
1.5kg finely minced pork to fill an 8in pie mould
200g minced bacon bits or anchovies (optional)
1 tsp salt
1 tsp white pepper
¼ tsp mace (optional)

Method

1 Mix all the filling ingredients together and chill in the fridge for 24hrs to allow the seasonings to permeate right through the mix.
2 Follow all the guidelines for the Game Pie recipe.

You can eat this pie warm as the French do, or cold as we English prefer. The reason for including the bacon is because it has been cured and contains nitrates that will help turn the pork pie meat pink. This can also be achieved by adding ground anchovies that carry a high percentage of natural nitrates and will not taint your meat mix with any kind of fish taste or smell.

Gala Pie

Made using the same pastry and meat mixture as the pork pie, but you do need a different pie mould. You need an anodised foldaway oblong veal and ham pie tin that has two sides, two ends and a bottom that slot together and sit on a base plate. A company called Silverwood of Birmingham makes these specialist tins.

Preparation time 45mins
Cooking time 90mins

Ingredients

7 medium free-range eggs
(hard-boiled)
Hot water pastry (follow recipe
on page 181) enough for
two tins
1kg forcemeat
Egg wash

Method

1 Grease the tin and then coat it in flour.

2 Hard-boil the eggs.

3 Take the pastry and use enough to hand raise within the tin until it reaches the top edge all the way round.

4 Place half the meat mix in the base of the pastry case.

5 Use a cold tablespoon to make a slight depression and channel in the meat to allow the eggs to sit in the centre without rolling away to the sides.

6 Top and tail the eggs so that the yolks can be seen at either end.

7 Place them all end-to-end down the centre of the pie in the channel.

8 Fill the remaining pork mix on top of the eggs.

9 Put a pastry lid on the pie, sealing and crimping the edges as you go.

10 Cook the pie as you would a game pie being sure to follow the guidelines for cooling and egg washing it to avoid a pastry collapse.

Ascot Pie

The same as Gala Pie but without the eggs.

TOP TIP

If you are going to sell these pies commercially, then it is of paramount importance to use gelatine. The reason for this is simple; as the gelatine enters the pie it forces the air out thus giving the pie a longer shelf life.

Pâté de Pâques (Easter Pie)

An unusual French pie that I came across in the Berry region of the Limousin in France. This pie is often made in a large 10in round cake tin, with a brioche pastry (recipe page 182) with a herb-based forcemeat, along with 6 hard-boiled eggs cut in half lengthways and placed flat side down on top of the forcemeat in a clock-face formation. This then acts as a slice guide, offering a portion of egg with every wedge sliced. The pie has a pastry lid and is baked in a preheated oven at 180°C for 60–90mins, or until golden brown.

Tourte Limousin

Les Tourtes Limousin (Limousin Pies) is a company based in the town of Bellac in the Haute Vienne of the Limousin region. This business was created by local *charcutier* Régis Bourdier whom I was privileged to meet on several occasions. Régis had heard I was in the area and sought me out to invite me to tour his new factory premises in Bellac. He explained to me that he had a successful family *charcuterie* business in the nearby town of Mézières-sur-Issoire where his family's creation, the *Tourte Limousin*, was selling by the thousand each week. His decision to build his new pie factory in Bellac ultimately meant he had to close the family's butchery shop, which had been in the town for more than a century.

These simple pies contained meat and potato or just simply potato (*pomme de terre*), thus demonstrating that the simplest of recipes if made well will serve you forever.

The *tourte* is composed of minced pork, sliced potatoes, sliced onion, double cream, chopped parsley, chopped tarragon, eggs, chopped chicken livers (optional) with salt and pepper to taste. This round pie normally has a brioche crust but short crust also works well. When making the *tourte*, remember to leave an overlap of pastry on both the base and the lid so that both edges can be folded and crimped together similar to a Cornish pasty. Once egg washed, the *tourtes* should be baked at 180°C for 50mins or until golden brown.

Régis Bourdier kindly offered me the use of his premises to make such products as Cornish pasties and steak and kidney puddings because I had given him several Ginsters® pasties from Cornwall and some puddings from Hollands Pies® in Lancashire. He somehow became confused by our conversation and he thought I was the creator of those products! My French was not good enough to explain to him that they were products that I had bought myself, but with hindsight I'm glad he thinks this about me – it would be dreadful of me to shatter his illusions. If Monsieur Bourdier thinks I'm the marvellous inventor of these products, I can live with that and raise my glass to him, "Chin, Chin!"

Oops! I must be careful with that expression for I know that "Chin Chin" means something completely different in Japanese.

Pork & Pippin Pie

Often referred to as a Cheshire pork pie, this dish has been around for centuries and is now made from many recipes. The main ingredient is diced or coarsely chopped pork with cubed apple seasoned with nutmeg, salt and pepper. Variations are found with both short crust and hot water pastry. You can of course mince the pork and add the diced apple with maybe some sliced onion and by including brown sugar you will bring all the flavours to the fore.

Huntingdon Fidget Pie

Made as the above but substituting diced bacon for the pork and adding some fresh sage.

If I were to open a pie shop in London today I think I would fix a red and white barber's pole above the door and call the business 'Mrs Lovett's Olde Pye Shoppe'. Do you think this would catch people's imagination?

OTHER MEATS

I n this chapter I will include recipes and information that do not fit comfortably into the other categories, but are important enough to be included in the book.

Comestibles prepared by Fortnum and Mason's famous London store were a popular request in the 1920s and 1930s. They often included such complex dishes as a Glazed Boar's Head, supplied decorated and ready to be placed as a centrepiece on the dining table in the grand homes of the rich and famous.

BEEF LOZENGES An invention for coach travellers, these were often taken into the Chamber by Members of Parliament to suppress their hunger pains during long sittings. Lozenges were probably made with a marrowbone reduction and bound together with molasses but sadly the original recipe is currently unavailable.

BEEF TEA Queen Victoria once ordered the store to supply 250lb of this in-house product, and asked for it to be sent to Florence Nightingale then based at Scutari in Turkey. To make your own, cook 1kg of lean beef in 1ltr of water and season with salt, when the beef is cooked the remaining juice can be used as beef tea. I find using salt beef gives a better flavour.

TURTLE SOUP Very popular in the 1930s, but when Fortnum and Mason's placed a live turtle in a large tank in their shop window to promote the in-house made soup it caused quite a stir and the company quickly found themselves in trouble and being raided by officers of the RSPCA.

Here are a few regional delicacies to tickle your taste buds.

SCOTCH PIE (MUTTON PIE) Originating in Scotland this short crust pasty has a mutton filling and firm pastry made from dripping. However it is not uncommon to find the pies made with a hot water pastry. The lid of the pie is set ½in lower than the rim to allow for a topping of gravy or potato and peas. These delicacies are sometimes referred to as 'Football Pies' due to their being sold at football grounds all over Scotland.

KATT PIE Yes, I said Katt not Cat. No, I'm not trying to catch you out, a dish that has its origins in Pembrokeshire, Wales. The pastry can be either a short crust or hot water one. It is filled with equal measures of mutton, currants and brown sugar with the addition of lemon zest and some thyme. Some recipes offer twice the amount of mutton as the other ingredients. A pork version of this pie also tastes very good and should perhaps be called a 'Welsh Pork Pie' (is nit).

Traditional Cornish Pasty

Serves 4
Preparation time 45mins
Cooking time 60mins

Ingredients

500g short crust pastry
   (recipe page 180)
500g raw beef (diced)
200g each of swede, potato,
   and onion (all raw and
   sliced)
Salt and pepper to taste
Egg wash

Ingredients can be varied
to include beef and Stilton,
beef and ale, pork and apple,
lamb and mint and bacon
and cheese.

Method

1 Having bought or made your pastry roll it out.
2 Place a 10in plate upside down on your pastry, cut all the way around the rim.
3 Use pastry disc as a casing to wrap your ingredients.
4 Place the raw ingredients: diced beef, sliced swede, potato and onion in a bowl and season with a little salt and a generous helping of pepper.
5 Place the mix on half of the pastry case, fold over the other half so the edges meet and crimp to hold shut.
6 Brush with beaten egg.
7 Cook in an oven preheated to 180°C for 45–60mins or until light golden in colour.

Clovelly Fish Pie

Yet more Cornish *charcuterie*, this time made with fish.

Serves 6–8
Cooking time 30mins
Preparation time 60mins

TOP TIP

Use mashed potato with cheese in lieu of short crust pastry if desired.

Ingredients

6 to 8 mackerel (gutted, de-boned and washed but with the heads still attached) *Mackerel can be oily so feel free to use an alternative fish*

500g short crust pastry (recipe page 180)

150g breadcrumbs

1 onion (finely chopped)

4 eggs (hard-boiled, chopped)

200g bacon lardons

Parsley or chives (chopped)

1 lemon

1 egg (beaten)

Milk and cream

Method

1 Gut, de-bone and wash 6 to 8 mackerel leaving the heads on.

2 Cover breadcrumbs with milk and allow to soak.

3 Add chopped parsley or chives with the juice and zest of a lemon mixed with finely chopped onion.

4 Add eggs and lardons.

5 Mix all the non-fish ingredients together.

6 Stuff the fish with the mixture.

7 Arrange fish and remaining mix around a greased pie dish, adding a little cream if you wish.

8 Make and roll out a short crust pastry lid for the pie dish.

9 Before sealing the pie, make several slits in the lid and pull through the fish so their heads are exposed.

10 Glaze pie with beaten egg.

11 Cook in a preheated oven at 180°C for 60mins, or until the pie is golden brown.

Steak Hache

In many ways similar to a burger but normally prepared on demand and contains no seasoning. It is very important to point out that a *Steak Hache* should be treated as a superior quality product and not as a burger, albeit the burger is its nearest relative.

Serves 4
Preparation time 30mins
Cooking time 6–8mins

Ingredients

500g beef

Method

1 Trim any sinews and gristle from prime cuts of meat.
2 Run through the coarse plate of a grinder once only.
3 Form into 125g patties using an ice cream scoop.
4 Place a knob of butter infused with herbs or garlic on top of the meat whilst cooking.
5 Best eaten fried or grilled medium rare with thick-cut chips.
6 If you prefer, prepare a cream sauce, choosing ingredients that will complement the meat such as wild mushrooms or blue cheese and walnuts.
7 Remember, unlike making burgers, it is the chef or cook who seasons a *Steak Hache* and not the butcher.
8 Finally, garnish with yet another knob of herb butter.

WHIST PIE Made from beef and short crust pastry and the size of a small narrow coffee cup, these pies can be found in Lancashire at markets such as the famous one in Bury. It is said these small savouries were eaten as snacks at whist games.

RAG PUDDING Another Lancashire delicacy made with suet pastry, often filled with pieces of beef skirt and sliced onion, but any meat can be used. Traditionally the raw ingredients would be placed in a pudding dish with a suet casing and lid or just a lid on its own. Then rags would be tied over the lid before it was steamed for 3 hours. Lancashire in times past had cotton mills as their main industry and from these mills came a plentiful supply of rags to cover these heavy puddings. Individual portions of a similar pudding made in a 'roly-poly' style can still be bought today from Jackson's Farm Fayre in Rochdale.

I once met the Hairy Bikers (Simon King and Dave Myers) at one of their 'Recipe Fair' events held at the Cotswold Farm Park in Gloucestershire. There I produced a rag pudding and a bacon roly-poly complete with vegetables and gravy. This was divided up and presented to the crowd for tasting and there was much fun and delight expressed in the finished dish.

I have to say here, that of all the celebrity chefs I have met over the years, the Hairy Bikers were the most generous in every way. I felt really at home with these guys but then, they are Northerners!

Pressed Beef

A tasty way to use up leftovers.

Method

1   Place all your scrap cuts of meat along with any available bones in a large stockpot or boiler.
2   Cover with water or stock and simmer for 6hrs or until the meat falls from the bones.
3   Shred all the meat fibres, season with salt and pepper.
4   Press in a terrine with gelatine and some stock.
5   Stand the terrine in a cool place for at least 24hrs, it will then be ready to slice and serve.

POTTED STEW A mixture of any combination of meats, but normally made with beef (30%), lamb (30%) and pork (40%), prepared like the pressed beef in a large stockpot or boiler with the addition of a little saltpetre to help preserve the meat. Gelatine is not normally added to this dish, and it is not pressed because this dish needs to be spreadable. Ideally served on bread with sliced raw onion.

The bear necessities

Jerky meat has its origins in the Northern States of the USA and Canada. In 1982 I found myself in Canada where I planned to seek out the Native American Indians and obtain some of their original jerky recipes. But first I had some military work to do as I was visiting this magnificent country with the Queens Lancashire Regiment, the QLRs (also known by other friendly army units as the 'Queen's Last Resorts' and sometimes the 'Queers, Lesbians and Rejects' – but sticks and stones eh? No matter what you call the QLRs they do hold more battle honours than any other British regiment and that makes them unique).

I was scheduled to be in Canada for 6 weeks carrying out various duties (some recreational), such as canoeing through the Rocky Mountains on the Saskatchewan River from near Jasper to Medicine Hat, whilst surviving on the wild for food. Finding food in the wild always seems to come easy to me, coming as I do from an agricultural background. Even as a young lad I could cut a length of a blackberry vine and use it to twist into small rabbit burrows or holes in stonewalls to catch rabbits. The twisted vine binds itself into the fur of a sitting rabbit so you can slowly pull out your furry feast. This and other rural skills kept me from going hungry on military exercises and such was my skill that other men would draw straws in order to team up with me, because they knew that if I was a team member their morale would remain high since they would never have an empty stomach.

Canoeing through the Rockies was certainly one of the highlights in my life. Seeing beavers trailing their cuttings to their dams and giant moose drinking at the water's edge whilst we silently floated by was magical. We even saw ospreys fishing; they would swoop down to the water and grab a salmon from the flowing river.

With bison grazing on the lush grasslands, we only needed David Attenborough and the scene would be complete – that is how it felt on that canoe trip. I was really getting excited because at the end of the exercise I was due a few days R&R that would enable me to visit the local Indians to ask about their jerky recipes and methods of preserving meat. I already knew they used whatever meat they could trap and would cut it into thin shreds and sometimes rub hedgerow herbs into it, prior to drying it on hot rocks in the sun. They would occasionally smoke meat high up within the tepee poles where there was a gap for the internal fire smoke to escape. Getting this information first-hand would be an absolute treat for me, and I could hardly contain my enthusiasm as I was also hoping to pass on my hunting and trapping skills to the Indians and to be taught some of their methods in return. (I did become a poacher turned gamekeeper for a while, but that's another story, or should I say another book, one that will cover hunting, shooting and fishing with recipes to whet your appetite!)

On the last night out with our canoes my colleagues and I had arranged to make camp and meet up on one of the islands in the river for a 'jolly' around a small campfire. Here we planned to share some beers and cook fish we had caught earlier in the day. We had just set our two-man tents with the openings facing inwards towards the campfire in order to benefit from the heat when suddenly we heard a rustling noise in the undergrowth! This made us all nervous as we were armed only with eating knives, because for some unexplained reason, the Canadian authorities did not trust us to be out in the wild with a firearm.

We had nothing to worry about however, since the noise was only a couple of Canadian men who had spotted our campfire from the river, and in the fading light had decided to use our already lit fire to cook their evening meal. We welcomed the men and they used the fire and thanked us with a six-pack of beer, which was most welcome. They did say that they were surprised to find us out there in the mountains with no firearms to protect ourselves from the local grizzly bears. (Yer right! What grizzlies?) The two men having been fed and having shared a tale or two decided to move on up-river to camp for the night away from our base camp. This was a surprise to us, but we did learn why a little while later.

Again another noise from the undergrowth! And this time we were not afraid as we thought it would be the two Canadians returning to our camp, but … Oh No! Not this time…. It was a huge, and I mean a really huge F*****G GRIZZLY, and we all did the same thing to protect ourselves from this huge, snarling, furry man-killer. Yes, we all zipped up our nylon tents! All you could hear was that familiar noise a zip makes when being closed Ziiiiiiiiiiiiiiiiiiiiiiip! Well of course a nylon tent would be no deterrent to a 7ft angry or hungry grizzly bear, but we just acted instinctively and that meant closing the door … and this door was a zipped nylon sheet! Having flown to Canada we carried no knives, not a Bowie, not even a simple pen knife, the only implements we had were our mess tins and diggers (knife, fork and spoon), so the only thing we could do was rattle and bang our mess tins together to make as much noise as possible. Thankfully the bear was more frightened than we were and scampered away through the trees (it may have been the smell of all that brown adrenalin) leaving us soldiers alive to learn from the experience. An additional lesson I learned was that we should have known that bears can smell food up to 5 miles away, so we should have eaten our quarry (i.e. the

fish) raw and *sushi*-style on that occasion to avoid creating a scent trail.

On the following morning I felt better than I had in a long while, one reason being that we all survived the grizzly bear's visit and another that I knew this was my last day on exercise, meaning I could be with the Indians that afternoon, sharing recipes and hunting techniques. We loaded up the canoes and got underway, making our way through some white water and rocks when all of a sudden we saw a stone bridge spanning the river ahead of us. On the bridge were several men frantically waving at us and shouting messages we could not decipher at first because the noise of the roaring white water was too loud. As we got closer we realised the men were from our unit and they were not shouting words of encouragement, they were flagging us down to stop. We managed to get ashore where our colleagues told us we were needed back in the UK ASAP. On asking why, we were informed there was a 'bit of trouble going on' that required our help. All the while and selfishly I was thinking: "This can't be happening, I'm off to find jerky recipes this afternoon and to spend time with the Native Indians, what on earth could be more important than that?". We were helped out of the water with all our gear and taken to Fort Wainwright in Alberta then onto the city airport in Edmonton before being flown back to the UK.

On the plane back to England I thought of my missed jerky venture and the night the grizzly bear visited our camp, "So close and yet so far away". The only thing I can do now is, to make a vow to myself to return another day! Oh by the way, that 'bit of trouble' that needed our help (remember this was 1982) yes, you are right, it turned out to be the Falklands War!

P.S. Have I told you about that recipe for Penguin Pie?

SALT BEEF (CORNED BEEF) Easily made using silverside, just wet-cure the meat as you would bacon or ham. The beef is better when it has been slowly boiled for several hours. Serve warm in a sandwich or over winter vegetables as a main course. When eaten cold it is also very tasty especially when served with mustard and baby *cornichons* (gherkins) along with a light salad and crusty bread.

Marrow Bone Butter

In my book this is the *crème de la crème* of all butters.

Method

1   Saw the ends off several marrowbones and place them on a baking tray.
2   Cook in an oven at 180°C for 50mins or until the marrow starts to melt.
3   Once the bone marrow has softened enough scoop it out of the bones.
4   Add unsalted butter and blend the two together.
5   Season the mixture and set in a ramekin.
6   The finished butter can be used on toast, to flavour meats or even to enrich a sauce; I enjoy it in risottos and as a dilution to blue cheese for steaks.

TRIPE Found in any animal; pig tripe is often used to make *Andouillette*. A cow's stomach lining makes delicious tripe and onions when cooked, but can also be eaten raw with lots of vinegar. Another way is to turn the tripe into a pouch, stuff it with forcemeat and bake it as a pâté or meatloaf that can be glazed and eaten either warm or cold.

Elder is the lining of the cow's udder and the only way I know how to eat this velvet-like meat is cold and with plenty of malt vinegar. Sheer bliss! Elder and raw tripe would often be sold on tripe stalls to the men suffering from a hangover, as they were deemed to provide so rapid a cure that sufferers were able to go straight back to the pub from the tripe stall and start another session. I remember one such place in the covered market in Burnley, Lancashire, where I would often see many men queuing for their 'fix' of tripe on a Saturday morning, but strangely I never saw them in the market place on a Monday morning!

Cow Heel

I think this is best used in a cow pie, where succulent pieces of blanched cow heel along with diced brisket make for the simplest of ingredients and yet produce an amazing pie.

Preparation time 4hrs
Cooking time 60mins

Ingredients

1kg beef (diced brisket)
2 cow heels
1 onion (sliced)
500g potatoes
Gravy
Salt and pepper to taste

Method

1 Simmer the heel for at least 3hrs in stock.
2 De-bone and chop the meat into bite-sized pieces.
3 Mix with slow-cooked brisket, raw potatoes and onion, season with salt and pepper.
4 Add gravy and place in a greased pie mould.
5 Cover with puff pastry and bake at 180°C or until cooked.
6 You can add ale or kidneys, or even mushrooms, to your ingredients if you so wish and all that is left now, is to invite your friend Desperate Dan to help devour this scrummy feast.

Mincemeat

Traditionally this should be started no later than October if you wish to use it for Christmas.

Ingredients for a 10kg mix

3kg beef brisket or a mix of tongue and brisket
1kg suet (minced or grated)
1kg currants
1kg raisins
1kg sultanas
1kg mixed peel
½kg marmalade

½kg brown sugar
2 tsps salt
2 tsps allspice
2 tsps cinnamon
2 tsps mace
2 tsps nutmeg
2 ltr brandy or a mix of brandy and sherry

TOP TIP

When boning and rolling breast of mutton, spoon some mincemeat onto the meat before rolling and tying, this adds a nice subtle flavour to the finished dish. When making mincemeat you could, if you wish, start with just 5% of meat and add more each time you make it until you reach the point that suits you best.

Method

1 Brine-cure meat(s)for 24hrs.
2 After curing, cook the meats in water on a low heat for 3hrs then leave to cool.
3 Peel the tongue and mince the meat on a coarse plate.
4 Mix all the ingredients together and store in a crock-pot until required.

Merguez

A fresh sausage originating from North Africa and usually made with just beef and mutton to suit people of the Muslim faith. The following recipe with the added pork has been developed to suit European tastes.

The shelf life of this sausage is between 5 and 7 days if kept refrigerated.

Preparation time 45mins

Ingredients

3kg beef	220g mild chilli powder
3kg pork	40g ground cumin
3kg mutton	50g garlic
180g salt	40g aniseed or
20g black pepper	crushed star anise
20g paprika	(both optional)
30g hot chilli powder	120ml olive oil

Method

1 Trim the meat of all sinews and tendons etc.
2 Mince the meat through a 5–6mm plate.
3 Add and blend the seasoning into the meat mix.
4 Fill 22–24mm diameter lamb casings to the length of your choice.

TOP TIP

This sausage can be pricked and sun-dried for 2 days and then stored in jars of olive oil until required. It is best to heat the oil before submerging the sausage in it. Adding sun-dried or char-grilled paprika flesh, bay leaves and garlic will add colour and a little mystery to the jar.

LAMB PANCETTA Is quite simply the breast of lamb, boned, rolled and dry cured for at least 10 days before it is air-dried for at least 3 weeks. I use it by thinly slicing and then cooked between two baking sheets until crispy. I then serve it as a crispy hard lid to a lamb hot pot served in a large ramekin. I serve dauphinoise potatoes alongside the ramekin.

MUTTON HAM Cured in the same way as any other meat, the joint is probably best tunnel-boned so that it can be sliced very thinly and served on an *Assiette de Charcuterie* with a green salad, quartered hard-boiled eggs, gherkins and a creamy horseradish sauce.

COLONIAL GOOSE A dish with New Zealand origins, this is mutton stuffed with a sweet filling and cooked and served with warm vegetables and gravy. It is called Colonial Goose in an attempt to hide the fact that mutton is once again on the menu! I stuff mine with my homemade mincemeat and it tastes great. You could go one step further and be inventive by making a Colonial Goose Surprise, use the same method but with a real goose in place of the mutton.

Lancashire Hot Pot

A sure way to please any family on a budget, this dish can hit the spot whether you are a prince or a pauper. I prefer de-boned meat in this dish but you can increase the meat content to 800g if you use such meat as scrag end of neck on the bone.

Preparation time 30mins
Cooking time 2–3hrs

Ingredients

500g mutton or lamb
  (de-boned, optional)
500ml stock
50g plain flour
25g butter
2 kidneys
1 Bury black pudding (optional)
1 *chorizo* or *merguez* sausage
  (chopped, optional)
2 onions
2 carrots
Salt and pepper

Method

1 Peel and slice the potatoes and leave half to one side.
2 Use the rest to line the bottom of a greased casserole dish.
3 Cut the onions into 6 and sweat them in the butter until soft but not brown, then place on top of the potatoes.
4 Peel and slice carrots and mix in with the onions.
5 Coat the meat in seasoned flour and brown in a skillet.
6 Add to the casserole dish along with sliced black pudding.
7 Season the dish, cover with the remaining potatoes and add the stock so that the potatoes are just slightly covered.
8 Cook in a hot oven at 180°C for approximately 2 to 3hrs.
9 Serve with chunky bread.

Stand by your plates!

Back in the early 1980s whilst I was still serving in the military, we were informed by our Sergeant Major that we were due a visit from the Colonel-in-Chief of our Regiment. Our Colonel-in-Chief is Her Majesty Queen Elizabeth II, and I was informed that I had just 'volunteered' along with some other soldiers to become a waiter and work the front-of-house in the Officers' Mess for her visit.

As you can imagine I was a quivering wreck at the thought I might be serving the Queen with an *aperitif* or with *hors d'oeuvres*. On recognising this terror our mentors informed us that we would undertake training over the next few weeks to ensure we understood how to manage silver service with the formal etiquette that was required for such a royal visit. We were taught many things over the next few weeks, such as how to address Her Majesty if spoken to, and how to lay a table, for we were to honour the Queen's visit with a Regimental Banquet (well, … OK … a nice midday meal).

After all the training was complete it was decided that a full rehearsal was required to finalise the arrangements and to give our Commanding Officer peace of mind for the real thing. You see, it was all about preparation, preparation, preparation! The visit was scheduled for a Friday, as was the practice for approximately 120 guests. It was mid-autumn and all the fallen leaves had been picked up, the green grass had been swept, the stonework on the driveway to the Officers' Mess had been painted bright white, police officers and dog handlers were checking all the manhole covers around the building, there was a buzz of excitement and this was only the practice day! Inside, the Officers' Mess was frantic with people doing all kinds of jobs: barmen were de-corking bottles of red wine; cleaners were vacuuming for the third time and polishing the regimental silver; we waiters were laying the banquet tables that were in the shape of an E – a top table and three double-sided aisles running from it. Eventually it was time to welcome the guests; everyone had been invited for the rehearsal, except for Her Majesty and her Lady-in-Waiting along with four other VIPs. The guests gathered around the Officers' Mess bar and lounge where drinks were poured readily and without a single incident so that everybody had a charged glass. Some time later after the gong had been sounded, all the guests moved through to the banquet room where the Regimental Band was playing and all sat down to the menu.

The meal was to be a simple three-course menu with a main course of Lamb Noisettes, which I am given to believe is one of the Queen's favourite dishes. We waiters were in our best uniform and kitted out with white cotton gloves for the occasion, we all rallied round the kitchen and then the tables to serve and collect all the plates from each course again and again like clockwork! It all went without a hitch, thanks to the preparation, preparation, preparation. Our CO was delighted and congratulated everyone for his or her efforts, all we had to do was wait a week and do it for real.

On the following Friday, the day of Her Majesty's visit, we first had to serve *aperitifs* in the Officers' Mess bar and lounge, I found myself with a tray of white wines and gin and tonics. Desperate to get a nod or even a 'Hello' from Her Majesty, I found myself walking sideways like a crab and slowly getting nearer. Not knowing what I would say if she approached, all the while thoughts of my intended speech were going through my head with none making any sense. One such thought was that I was going to inform her that I once had a crush on her daughter, however the thought of being thrown into the Tower as a bleeding nutter stopped me making that remark! Just when I was about to ask her if she would like a fresh G&T, an officer swooped the last remaining full glasses from my tray and ordered me to go and help out in the kitchen! Gutted I was, proper gutted; my stalking skills were not good enough that day. Also, on this day, there was more top brass around than ever before and people were dishing out unnecessary orders. One of those new last-minute orders was for all us waiters to take off our white cotton gloves and to serve the food without them. For me that was fine, but some of those hardened soldiers had such awful tattoos as 'Love' and 'Hate' across their knuckles and this was now going unnoticed – but it was too late and we were underway with the meal. We had to keep an eye on our Sergeant who was the headwaiter and whose job it was to look after the Her Majesty, for we could not serve nor take away a plate until he had served the Queen first. This was not a problem on practice day, but today we had a new recruit with us – a Scouser with 'those' tattoos on his knuckles. He had seen our Sergeant take away the Queen's plate, so he thrust himself behind one of the elegant lady guests and insisted she cleared her unfinished plate in his best 'scouse speak', "C'mon lar gerrit down yer neck lar" whilst grappling for her plate with his tattooed hands!

We also noticed that the two people on the end of each aisle were not getting a meal, for the Cook Sergeant had forgotten to add on the six placements that were not at the practice day. Thankfully some of the behind-the-scenes staff had not eaten and gave up their lunch in order that these guests could eat without Her Majesty noticing that anything was wrong. So much for all that preparation, preparation, preparation... because if you cannot count then you are in trouble! Our regimental motto is 'Loyally I Serve' and this day proved to be just that. Serving Her Majesty as both a soldier and a waiter was a highlight in my military career.

Did you know? That a Capon is a male chicken that has been castrated at a young age, this then produces a bird with tender meat that will usually be heavier than a standard broiler. When I was living in France, I would sell many of these birds at Christmas time. Often people would come to the shop and ask me "Have you a Capon?", I would reply "No, I'm just wearing a baggy shirt today".

GESIERS (GIZZARDS) Duck or chicken gizzards are superb when heated with lardons and used as a scattering over a salad, however when they are sliced they lend themselves particularly well to an omelette for adding both taste and colour and to finish the dish with a little chopped parsley.

Prosciutto di Anatra

This Italian product is one of my favourites, for it involves breasts, yes, that is right, or to be more precise, duck breasts.

Method

1 Take a whole duck, remove the breasts.
2 Dry cure for 3 days using a sweet cure (see page 84).
3 Hang cured breasts to air-dry for at least 7 days after which they are ready to use.
4 Ideally serve thinly sliced and eaten raw like *carpaccio*.

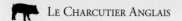

Confit de Canard

Made from the duck carcass after the breasts have been removed.

Serves 2
Preparation time 12hrs including curing time
Cooking time 2hrs

Method

1 Take off the legs complete with the thighs.
2 Cure for 12hrs using a sweet dry cure (see page 84).
3 No need to pre-heat the oven, just cook the legs until brown and the meat starts to shrink off the bone.
4 Remove from the oven to cool.
5 Once cooled, place the legs in a tall Kilner® jar, top up with duck fat and store in a cool larder until required.

Rillette de Canard

Preparation time 30mins
Cooking time 4–6hrs

Ingredients

500g duck meat
500g pork meat
500g pork fat
100ml water
Salt and pepper
Nutmeg
Thyme

Use the same method as
  Rillette de Porc (page 139).

Q: Do you know that the "quack" of a duck cannot echo? True or False?

A: True

RILLETTE D'OIE Exactly as above, with goose meat rather than duck.

DUCK *JUS* Made from the remaining duck carcass by crushing the skeleton in a duck press and saving the juice in an ice cube tray in the freezer until needed.

GRATTONS The duck equivalent to pork scratchings, can be made easily by cutting the remaining duck skin into bite-sized pieces and cooking them in a hot oven until brown and crispy.

Q: How do you sex ducks?
A: Some species of duck can be easily sexed by their plumage; the drakes being more colourful than the ducks. Drakes can often have a curled tail feather, but be warned, as some farmers will pluck this feather and try and pass off the drake as a duck in order to get a higher price. However the best way to sex a live duck especially whilst young is to grab them by their necks and lift them off the ground, a duck will quite clearly quack and a drake will rasp the (q)uack and most definitely without the Q and sounding as if it has a sore throat.

Frogs

Best deep-fried.

Method

1 Take the back legs off the frog and dispose of the rest, as it is too tricky to use.
2 Coat the legs in plain flour seasoned with salt and pepper.
3 Make a light batter (see page 184) using beer or a sparkling white wine.
4 Add chopped parsley or coriander with maybe a little lemon zest.
5 Dip the legs in batter and deep fat fry, for approximately 4mins or until golden brown.

SNAILS Once de-shelled, can be cooked in exactly the same way as the frog's legs with the cooking time reduced to 3mins. Good used as a topping to a salad or warmed through without the batter in a skillet of garlic butter with some chopped parsley.

Rabbit

Versatile and used in many forms such as a *Rillette de Lapin* made just as you would with pork, duck or goose, you will, of course, have to add pork fat and follow the recipe for *Rillette de Porc*. Using rabbit in a game pie works well especially as a contrast to dark meats and a rabbit and creamy leek pie tastes just sublime.

Skinning and preparing a wild rabbit

1 Hold the rabbit in both hands with its belly facing upwards and the head facing towards you.

2 With your thumbs lightly press down into the sternum and stroke your thumbs towards the back legs, this will dispel any urine left in the bladder. (Allow your hunting dog, if you have one, to lick the urine as it will intensify the senses in your dog's nose the next time you are out hunting for rabbit.)

3 Place the rabbit on a chopping board and chop off the 4 feet.

4 Use a sharp knife or a pair of scissors to make an incision into the loose skin near the genitals and cut up towards the neck of the rabbit whilst avoiding cutting through the diaphragm or any internal organs.

5 Now pull the rear legs through the skin, so you can pull the skin right down the length of the body.

6 Pull the front legs through the skin and allow the skin to fall over the head.

7 With the neck now exposed cut through the bone and dispose of the skin and head.

8 Taking care, cut through the diaphragm and take out the intestines saving any giblets for stock.

9 You will now see a small tract left between the rear legs, insert your little finger and push out any remaining 'currants'.

10 Finish by rinsing the carcass under a cold tap and patting it dry ready for use.

Getting in a stew over Rick

Rabbit Stew or Hop-Pickers Stew to be precise was a dish I once cooked for Rick Stein and members of his film crew. You see, when I was living in Herefordshire on a hop farm, I was asked by Rick's team if he could pay us a visit on his tour of Britain as he was interested in the hops and the products we produced and had a particular interest in hop asparagus (sometimes known as hop shoots or even *jets de houblon* in the culinary world). Well, the day came, he arrived on a bright sunny Sunday morning complete with his entourage, we met at Ledbury railway station, and after the formal greeting and handshakes we all travelled in convoy down to the farm.

Rick and his team wasted no time at all and quickly went about their filming business. They filmed Rick in one of the fields hop tying with one of the farm workers and again at my neighbour's farmhouse where he cooked up some treats on the Aga using the hop asparagus. My neighbours Jill and John whose farm we were visiting, as they had the earliest crop of hops, also allowed us to use their garden to cook Rick and his team a working lunch. It had been decided I would cook them an all-in-one pot dish and that this would be an original Hop-Pickers Stew from the days when pickers travelled down from the Midlands to harvest the hops.

Into the pot went many portions of (ferret-caught) rabbits that had been in a mustard and cider marinade overnight. Added to the pot were local ingredients that included potatoes, celery, carrots, swede, and large lardons of dry-cured bacon all covered with a chicken stock. I cooked this dish on a 'fire devil' i.e. an elongated brazier for want of a better description, a rail ran across and above the fire devil and from it pots and pans were hung on chains just above the heat, which was generated from wood gathered around the farm.

I recall this massive pot being totally emptied by the film crew; David Pritchard, who was Rick's Producer, had at least three helpings and then went on to mop up the dregs with some farmhouse bread! Just before the lunch started, Rick was being filmed with Jill cooking the hop asparagus on the Aga in her large traditional farmhouse kitchen. I was outside with Jill's husband John when the telephone rang; it was his daughter who asked him, "Can I speak to Mum?". John answered, "I'm sorry dear your mother is tied up at the moment, she's in the kitchen cooking some asparagus with Rick Stein". You could hear his daughter laughing on the phone whilst protesting to her father and asking him to hand over the phone to her mother. John stood firm and again explained she was in the kitchen cooking with Rick Stein. The conversation stopped and I saw that John was looking blankly at the cordless handset; for it was obvious his daughter had put the phone down on him. Well, about 10mins later a car rolled down the farm drive and you could hear doors slamming, children's voices, and the muttering of an adult female, this muttering got louder and louder as it approached us in the garden, when suddenly from around the corner of the house John's daughter appeared and protesting to her father that he was acting foolishly. Realising I was there she paused for a moment to wish me "Good day", before asking again "Now where is Mum? I need a word". Before John could say anything the film crew came out of the house followed by Jill and Rick Stein. That poor girl did not know whether to laugh or cry, or even both! Her face truly was a picture, she was gasping for air and pointing to her mother saying nervously "That's, that's, that's ... Rick Stein! What's Mum doing with Rick Stein?" Candid camera at its best that moment was!

Terrine of Wild Rabbit (*Terrine de Lapin*)

Welcome any time of the year; when accompanied by fresh bread and salad this makes an ideal starter or light meal.

Preparation time 45mins
Cooking time 75–90mins

Ingredients

1 wild rabbit (de-boned)
Mixed chicken livers and belly pork in equal amounts
  to that of rabbit
Enough slices of streaky bacon to line a terrine mould
2 garlic cloves (crushed)
2 sprigs of thyme
1 zest of a lemon
1 juice of a lemon or ½ glass of dry white wine

TOP TIP

You can add more rabbit than liver and pork, or even add whole pieces of rabbit meat to give a real rustic feel to the dish.

Method

1 Line the terrine with slices of streaky bacon.

2 Using a blender, make a runny mix of the chicken livers.

3 Add the remaining meats and grind to a coarse mix.

4 Place the mix on top of the bacon slices and seal.

5 Stand the terrine in a *bain-marie* and cook in an oven pre-heated to 180°C for about 80mins or until cooked through.

6 Once cooked allow to cool, place weights on top of the terrine and chill for at least 24hrs before use.

Rillette de Lapin

When made correctly offers a blend of meat and fat that is beyond belief, so go on, give it a go!

Preparation time 60mins
Cooking time 4–6hrs

Ingredients

6kg rabbit meat (8kg including bones)
2kg belly pork (diced)
2kg pork dripping
150g salt
10g white pepper
5g nutmeg

TOP TIP

Cover the *rillette* with 2cm of fat if you wish to store for any length of time.

Method

1 Melt the dripping in a large stockpot with 20ml of water and bring to a high heat.

2 Place the meat into the pot and reduce to a low heat.

3 Sprinkle the salt over the meat.

4 Leave to simmer gently for 4hrs then add the pepper and nutmeg.

5 Cooking for a further hour, or until the meat falls of the bones.

7 Take the meat out of the pot and shred.

8 Having removed all the bones, fold the meat back into some of the cooking fat until it achieves your preferred consistency.

9 Pot the *rillette* into glass jars or ceramic pots.

This recipe also works well with squirrel!

Rabbit in Pastry (*Lapin en Croute*)

Often known as 'Rabbits in Burrows' or 'Rabbit Wellington' these 'sausage rolls' undeniably surprise all those lucky enough to try them, and introducing children to eating rabbit this way doesn't come any easier.

Preparation time 45mins
Cooking time 20–30mins

Ingredients

1 packet of ready-made puff pastry

2 large wild rabbits

Belly pork to equal the weight of the rabbit meat minus the loins

Beaten egg

Seasoning, 1kg salt with 50g white pepper, mix well and then use at a ratio of 20g per kilo of finished meat (store the remainder in an airtight container for later use). Add green herbs of your choice: chervil, dandelion, chives, sage, sorrel, thyme or tarragon etc to taste.

Method

1 Carefully remove the loin meat from the rabbits and reserve.

2 Pare off all other rabbit meat and mince with equal amounts of belly pork to obtain a fine mix.

3 Add the required seasoning and mix well.

4 Roll out the pastry and divide into strips about 12–15cm wide.

5 Using a piping bag, force the meat onto the centre of the pastry and pipe from one end to the other.

6 With the back of a tablespoon, make a slight indentation along the mix.

7 Place the reserved rabbit loins along the mix and cover with another layer of forcemeat. Brush the pastry edges with an egg wash and fold over and crimp the two edges together.

8 Cut the roll into equal lengths and then score with a knife.

9 Bake in a pre-heated oven at 180°C for 20mins or until golden brown.

TOP TIP

Adding ½ tsp water to an egg wash makes it easier to use.

Jugged Hare

Can be cooked and stored in large Kilner® jars ready to be reheated when required during those cold winter nights.

Preparation time 45mins
Cooking time 2–3hrs

Ingredients

1 hare
8 small shallots
150g lardons
2 carrots
2 celery stalks
1 *bouquet garni*
1 large knob of butter
1 tbsp plain flour
250ml port
1 zest of a lemon
Salt and pepper

Method

1   Cut the hare into manageable pieces and coat in seasoned flour.

2   Brown in a skillet and place in a large casserole dish.

3   Cover the meat with water, add the lardons, shallots, diced carrots, diced celery, lemon zest and *bouquet garni*.

4   Cook for 2–3hrs at 160°C or until the meat is tender enough to fall off the bones.

5   Melt the butter in a skillet and add the flour, pour in the port and thicken.

6   Add some of the cooking juice and season with salt and pepper.

7   Fill Kilner® jars and top up with the cooking juices if necessary.

8   Serve with potatoes and red cabbage.

TOP TIP

Using the blood of the hare will enrich the gravy for this dish.

PS: A chef I know, once mistakenly used daffodil bulbs instead of shallots for this dish, these being poisonous he was rushed to the local casualty department immediately for medical attention. When I arrived at the hospital to visit him, the doctor said he was seriously ill, but he would recover and be out in the Spring. Gotcha!

Carpaccio of Cured Venison

The pinnacle of all *carpaccio*, served thinly sliced and laid on a platter to tease the taste buds of unsuspecting guests before they move on to a main course. You could argue cured meat cannot be used as *carpaccio*, but I would say; "So long as we are not cooking the meat then we are within the boundaries". First choose your cut of meat; loins and tenderloins work best. Next, dry cure the meat and seal it in a vacuum bag – if you do not have a vacuum packer just use a zip-lock type bag.

Sweet Dry Cure Mix

6kg salt

3.2kg brown sugar

800g saltpetre

Add such herbs as crushed juniper berries, thyme, bay leaves or marjoram

Use 50g per kilo of meat

Method

1 Assuming you are using a piece of loin about 4in long, cure it for 5 days in the fridge, turning daily.

2 At the end of the curing time, remove from the bag, pat dry with a paper towel and it is ready for use.

3 For a mature taste put the meat back into the fridge to air-dry for 7–10 days. (Leaving it to air-dry for longer will result in a *Bresaola*.)

4 Slice thinly and serve with a caper vinaigrette or a simple dressing of olive oil.

5 Enjoy!

Venison Rolled in Biltong

Quick, simple and very enjoyable.

Preparation time 15mins
Cooking time 15mins

Method

1   Cut a piece of venison loin 6cm long or butcher the hindquarters to cut off a pave (square piece).

2   Using a micro-blade, grate some biltong onto a chopping board, then rub olive oil into the piece of meat before rolling the loin firmly on the board to coat with the biltong.

3   If using a pave, just coat 4 sides leaving the two ends clear.

4   Seal the meat in a hot heavy pan with a little oil.

5   Cook in an oven pre-heated to 180°C for 8mins (rare), 10mins (medium) or longer (well done). Ovens may vary, so use this as a guide only!

6   Once cooked, cover with foil and leave the meat to rest for at least 10mins.

7   Whilst the meat is resting make a Jaeger sauce.

8   Serve with *dauphinoise* potatoes, cooked red cabbage and a little sorrel as a dressing.

TOP TIP

If you don't fancy biltong, then roll in cracked pepper, maybe adding a little coarse sea salt and freshly chopped sage.

Jaeger Sauce

No better accompaniment to cooked loin of venison than this rich sauce – so when you feel like spoiling someone, try this.

Preparation time 15mins
Cooking time 15mins

Ingredients

1 ltr water
200g Knorr® Classic Pepper Sauce
400g button mushrooms (halved)
12 silverskin onions (optional)
200ml *crème fraîche* or double cream
100g butter

Method

1   Melt the butter in a heavy pan and cook the mushrooms and onions.

2   Bring the water to a boil in a separate pot and add the pepper sauce.

3   Whisk thoroughly and reduce to a simmer for a further 2–3mins.

4   Add the sauce to the mushrooms and onions and mix well.

5   Slowly add the *crème fraîche* to reach a rich consistency.

6   Spoon the sauce over or around the cooked game.

TOP TIP

Instead of the Knorr® sauce, you could de-glaze the pan with your favoured liquor and then add the remaining ingredients. Don't forget to use a little flour with the butter to thicken the sauce if required.

Venison Sausage

A deer carcass provides more meat trim than most other animals, so you need to be inventive as well as traditional when thinking how to butcher the meat. I find it useful and more efficient to take out the primal cuts along with the loins as this is by far the best approach to such lean animals. This then leaves the scrag and trim around the remaining carcass to make such things as sausage.

Preparation time 30mins

Ingredients

2kg venison
1kg belly pork
500g rusk
500ml vegetable stock (cold)
60g salt and pepper
20g fresh green herbs (chopped)

Method

1 Soak sausage skins overnight (34mm boar casings are best).
2 Mince the meats through a coarse plate.
3 Add the seasoning (except green herbs), pour in the vegetable stock and run through the grinder once more.
4 Mix in the green herbs to a good consistency.
5 Fill the casings, link to the required length and hang in the fridge for at least 12hrs before use.

TOP TIP

For a more earthy flavour add 500g of mixed venison pluck. Substitute the rusk with breadcrumbs or oatmeal or a mix of both.

Venison Burger

Venison has a unique flavour of its own and it is best to allow the flavour of the meat to be prominent, so build up the seasoning to a level that suits both your taste and that of those who may share in it.

Preparation time 30mins

Ingredients

1kg venison (fatty if possible)
2 large onions
Salt and pepper to taste

Method

1 Grind the venison and onions together and season with salt and pepper.
2 Use a ratchet ice cream scoop to lift 125g portions from the container.
3 Release and press into 4in discs.
4 Chill for at least 4hrs before grilling to allow the seasoning to permeate the meat.

TOP TIP

This particular recipe can also be used with pork to make German Frikadellen, that can be eaten hot or cold.

Alternative seasonings

Try this recipe with breadcrumbs, egg, onion, salt and pepper, paprika, parsley, mustard, oregano, garlic and Worcester sauce, added to your liking and then test cook until you reach a level you enjoy.

Osso Bucco

Serves 4
Preparation time 45mins
Cooking time 2–3hrs

Ingredients

4 veal shank steaks about
    50mm thick complete with
    the marrowbone
2 large carrots
2 celery stalks
2 small onions
8 garlic cloves
500ml red wine
2 ltr chicken stock
1 *bouquet garni*
1 tin chopped tomatoes
Plain flour for coating

TOP TIP

Use a gremolada of finely chopped parsley, grated lemon zest and the juice of one lemon spooned over the veal.

Method

1   Cook the veal steaks as for a Lancashire Hot Pot.
2   Season the steaks.
3   Dip them in flour then brown on both sides.
4   Remove from the pan and place to one side.
5   Chop carrot, celery and onion.
6   Add to the pan and soften slightly with some garlic.
7   Pour in the red wine to de-glaze the pot and reduce.
8   Replace the meat then add chicken stock, a *bouquet garni* and chopped tomatoes.
9   Cook in an oven preheated to 170ºC for 2–3hrs.
10 Once cooked, remove the *bouquet garni*, blitz the sauce in a blender and pour sauce over the dish.
11 Serve the meat with accompaniments of your choice.

HORSE Not easily found here in the UK as meat, however in both Germany and France there are specialist butchers who trade only in horsemeat. This dark rich meat is cooked and treated just like any good piece of beef. I have eaten horse-meat on several occasions and I find it at its best after having been hung for several weeks and then used 'blue' or even medium rare. But I can't recall Graham Kerr ever using this meat on his cookery programme! Did you get the joke? No! He was known as the Galloping Gourmet, oh my!

PASTRY

A *Charcutier* has an extensive repertoire and amongst his long list of products, he/she will undoubtedly include pastries of many kinds; some will be light and delicate like filo while others are heavy and doughy. In France the *Charcutier* can call upon the services of the local patisserie and boulangerie when large quantities of pastries or dough are required. However if you do have to make your own pastry here are some basic recipes for you to follow, and with them I give you the same advice as for all my recipes: "Remember they are only a guide and if you don't like the way I do it, then don't whinge about it, just change it around to suit your needs – that's the best way to achieve success. I won't be offended if you don't follow my recipe, I'll go so far to say, if you better one of these recipes then drop me a line and tell me what you did differently. Not only am I willing you to enjoy and be successful at what you do, but also I am always prepared to learn something myself". (You have probably worked out from those sentiments that pastry-making is a weakness of mine, well, you are right and I wasn't put off!)

Short Crust Pastry (*Pâté Brisée*)

Makes two 10in flans or 20 mini tarts.

Ingredients

450g plain flour
250g butter
100ml water
½ tsp salt

Method

1   Sieve the flour and add the salt.
2   Mix in the butter and work with your hands until you achieve a breadcrumb-like finish.
3   Add the water and form the pastry into a ball.
4   Keep in the bowl covered with a tea towel until required.

Puff Pastry (*Pâté Feuilletée*)

A rich and light pastry and is ideal for savouries.

Will make two-dozen (26) *vol-au-vents*. (No, no, no, not 24, remember a bakers dozen?)

Ingredients

450g plain flour
450g butter
300ml water
½ tsp salt

Method

1   Sieve the flour and add the salt.
2   Mix in 50g of the butter and work with your hands until you achieve a breadcrumb-like finish.
3   Add the water and form the pastry into a ball.
4   Roll out the pastry and do the same with the butter between cling film.
5   Place the butter on top of the pastry in the centre and bring in all four corners of your pastry to meet in the middle covering the butter.
6   Roll out the pastry again and fold into three.
7   Leave to chill for 30mins and repeat the process 5 or 6 times more.
8   The pastry is now ready to use.

Hot Water Pastry (*Pâté a Pâté*)

Mainly used for pork and game pies. Will make one large round pork pie using an 8in diameter pie mould. Please try this recipe before you decide on any changes, it really is that good!

Ingredients

500g plain flour
100g lard
100g butter
200ml water
2 tsps salt
2 eggs
Egg wash

Method

1 Sieve the flour and add salt and eggs.
2 Mix together and make a well in the middle for the liquid mix.
3 Slowly melt butter and lard in the water, do not boil.
4 Add to the pastry mix and bind together.
5 Cover and store overnight but not in the fridge.

Suet Pastry

This simple pastry, very familiar in my youth, is one of the most delightful because you know the casing will soon expose an inner treasure.

Will make two 6in pudding moulds.

Ingredients

500g self-raising flour
350ml water
300g suet
2 tsps salt

Method

1 Sieve the flour and add the salt.
2 Stir in the shredded suet and add the water until the mix reaches a soft dough texture.
3 Quickly knead and roll out the pastry and use it immediately, remembering a good thickness is required to stand steaming.

Dumplings

Serves 4

Ingredients

100g self-raising flour
50g suet shredded
Salt and pepper to taste
Water

Method

1   Add water to the mix until all the ingredients are combined, then roll into balls to the size you require.

2   Place the dumplings in your broth at least 30 minutes from the end of the cooking time to allow the ingredients to cook and swell.

Brioche Pastry

A French favourite, but one I could never accustom myself to using or eating, as it is far too sweet for me – I'm more of a savoury person.

Ingredients

175g plain flour
200g butter
3 tbsps sugar
2 tsps milk
2 egg yolks
1 sachet dried yeast
½ tsp salt

Method

1   Sieve the flour and add the salt and sugar.

2   Warm up the milk and yeast together and pour over the mix.

3   Add the eggs.

4   Knead the mixture to obtain a smooth, elastic dough.

5   Cover with a tea towel and let it rise for at least 8hrs.

Pizza Dough

So common, today's generation think it originated in the High Street or in a take-away. I sometimes feel there should be a culinary questionnaire given to customers who enter such premises to ensure they only eat if they correctly answer questions on the origins of the menu!

For one pizza base

Ingredients

350g strong white flour
200ml warm water
2 tbsps olive oil
1 tbsp dried yeast
1 tsp salt

Method

1 Add the yeast to the warm water along with the olive oil and leave to go frothy.
2 Sieve the flour with the added salt and add the frothy mix.
3 Bring together to make dough.
4 Knead until the dough becomes elastic.
5 Leave the dough in a bowl covered with a tea towel to prove for about 1hr.
6 When it has almost doubled in size it will be ready to use.

Yorkshire Pudding

More of a batter than a pastry, however I think this chapter is the best place for it. There are several recipes, but the one I remember most is one that is used by celebrity chef Brian Turner, a fellow Northerner, to whom I'll attribute this recipe since I cannot recall when or where I began using it.

Method

1 Using a teacup, measure equally 1 cup plain flour, 1 cup of whisked eggs and 1 cup of milk with a pinch of salt and pepper.
2 Mix together and leave to stand whilst you heat up your pudding tray with a dollop of dripping in each depression.
3 When the dripping begins to smoke add your mix and cook in the oven at 220°C for 25 to 30mins.

Batter is made easily by following the above Yorkshire Pudding recipe, however it would benefit from exchanging the milk for fizzy water or even beer to get air into the mix. This will then make the batter light and flavoursome.

Filo Pastry

A specialist craft and a pastry I have never attempted to make, so sadly I have no recipe to offer, only good advice. If you do not have a *patisserie* close by then ask at your local hotel if they have a pastry chef who can supply you with fresh filo, failing that some good supermarkets may sell it and almost certainly a good delicatessen will.

Choux Pastry

Remembered by my cousin Kelly Turner who, whilst reading my manuscript, called and in a mild panicky voice said "You've forgotten to mention choux pastry". I quickly replied explaining I do not use choux pastry in my repertoire, so therefore I have not included one. She went on to say just because I don't use it, others might, so therefore I ought to mention it in the book. For those of you who know Kelly, you know she can go on and on and on so "There, I have now mentioned choux pastry in this chapter, now you can stop ringing me Kelly, the book is finished!" Hope I don't forget to mention her in the acknowledgements or I'll never hear the last of it.

"Kelly I said I mentioned it, I did not say I had written a recipe. NOW GET OFF THE BLOODY PHONE!" I don't belieeeeve it. She's just like Victor Meldrew, she's just been on the phone again to tell me her name is spelt KELLIE and not Kelly.

SUMMARY

H opefully having read part of this book, if not the whole book, you will refer again to the chapters that have given you some enjoyment. I have tried my best to write this book in a fashion that makes easy reading, with buckets of humour and laughter, along with recipes that may tempt you to try without fear of failure or to doubt as to whether you are capable of the art of *charcuterie*.

I have purposely avoided long, complicated and formal recipes where science is dominant and where years of experience are required for their execution. Instead I have chosen basic recipes on which you can build a base from which to work, ones that hopefully will offer you the most fun with relatively speedy results, as I know for certain you will share your success with your friends and family and to great applause.

Some of the products listed in these chapters could fill a volume in their own right, for example, sausages, terrines and pâtés. Each has enough history, technique and variation to make three separate books. However, I hope with what I have covered I have not just explained the basics, but shared enough information to allow you to expand your repertoire in a direction prompted by your own personal taste.

I could have included a chapter on Environmental Health in relation to producing food products safely, however as each geographical area has its own Environmental Office with different interpretations of European guidelines it is better for you to approach your local office for advice. I have worked across Europe and in many counties here in the UK and have had to take a different approach in each and every controlling area.

For example, in Germany I had to send regular poo samples through the post to my local Environmental Office for analysis. This common German practice I always found a little strange, but it does demonstrate the differences in culture (no pun intended). One office here in the UK, that I will refrain from naming, had officers who constantly gave out conflicting advice to the extent that food business owners complained furiously and demanded they all sang from the same hymn sheet. So, given the complexity of this subject, my advice to you is to contact your local office and if your work carries you over borders into other controlling areas then you have my sympathy!

All the recipes I have offered are to be used as guides only and not as exact rulings, you must change, add or delete anything that pleases you, I don't want to hear you whingeing if you don't like something, remember tastes differ. I like salty bacon, my wife does not, I like French style high meat-content sausages, my wife does not, I like a chipolata – my wife said she had no choice! (What **did** she mean?)

It would please me to know that you have sharpened your pencil and made notes on aspects of this book and if you have really discovered a method that improves on anything I have shared with you, I expect you to contact me and let me know.

Talking about contacting me, will those Hollywood Film Producers who are reading this book and who wish to turn me into a film epic then please contact me via my agent.

"Flipping heck Kellie, no you can't be my agent, no we're not going to Hollywood it was a joke, a point of humour to finish the book, yes, yes I promise to tell you if someone calls!!"

Ring ring . . . . ring ring . . . . , "OMG! Kellie, quick, answer the phone it might be Hollywood !"

INDEX

USEFUL CONTACTS

BUTCHERY SUPPLIES

www.weschenfelder.co.uk

www.sausagemaking.org

www.mkingredients.co.uk

COOKERY SCHOOLS

www.empirefarm.co.uk

ww.thymeatsouthrop.co.uk

www.rivercottage.net

GENERAL SITES

www.sausagefans.co.uk

ACKNOWLEDGEMENTS

Well, where do I begin? On starting this book, I genuinely thought I could not reach past the first page given my phobia with the written word and yet I'm now here towards the end paying tribute to all those who have played a part. I've tried where possible to credit those people who have contributed to the book at the place and chapter of reference, as for the rest and in no particular order or preference I list those I thank, for you know how you have helped and forgive me if I miss anyone.

Annemarie – (I love you dearly) my wife and number one critic who has never been afraid to say when I had made something which tasted awful.

Daniel, Tanja, Kara, Melanie and Samuel the best kids one could ask for and to whom I dedicate this book.

George, my dad who has long since past away (1997), albeit dead he contributed through my memories. Thank's Dad.

Mike Smales, Simon Orpen, Linda Isaacson, Andy Seatherton, Severnview Farm Gloucestershire, Franck & Jude Pontais, Simon Hulstone of the Elephant Restaurant Torquay, Andy Harvey, Steve Mills, Phill Gadd, Rob Creber of Tavistock, Tim Weschenfelder of www.weschenfelder.co.uk, David Hammond (Captain retired, Army Catering Corp), Ben Creese Country Butcher Gloucestershire, Mike & Felicity Robinson, Clifford (Gill) Perkins, Jonathan Coates, Sally & Adrian Morgan, Stephen Plume of www.sausagefans.co.uk, Frank Miller, Sue Hainsworth, Franco Sotgiu of www.sausagemaking.org, Mark Smeed. Catherine Hollingworth, Tracy Staskevich and Tina Clarke of Pentacor.

Photo and illustration acknowledgements:

p.32 South Yeo Farm East for the Devon Black Pig, Frank Miller of www.britishloppig.org.uk for the Devon Lop Pig; p.48 Alice de Jong.

© Fotolia.com all images copyright: p.10 Dauf; p.11 Asymetria; p.18 Delphimages; p.27 Surlaplanet; p.40 yoh4nn; p.44 Jaques Palut; p.45 creative; p53 Dawn; p.56 babsi_w; p.62 Marco Mayer; pp.63, 130, 150, 188 Comugnero Silvana; p.65 Friday; p.111 bierchen; p.116 shaiith; p.120 Art_man; p.125 Jaroslaw Adamczyk; p.129 JJAVA; p.136 msheldrake; p.137 guy; pp.146, 178 Monkey Business; p.171 igor kisselev.

Shutterstock p34 © Antonio V. Oquias.

All illustrations by David Shenton www.davidshenton.com except pp.17, 20 Andrew Seatherton.